Supporting Language and Communication

This series of books is written for more experienced Teaching Assistants (TAs) who may be studying for a Foundation Degree or working towards HLTA status. Each book looks at how to approach your role as professionally as possible, gives you the advice and guidance you need in order to improve your skills as you progress and most importantly contains contributions from your peers, as TAs themselves write about their own best practice.

Titles in this series:

Claire Taylor, Min Wilkie and Judith Baser: Doing Action Research

Rosemary Sage: Supporting Language and Communication

Min Wilkie, Tricia Neal and Doug Dickinson: Supporting ICT

Ashley Compton, Helen Fielding and Mike Scott: Supporting Numeracy

Supporting Language and Communication

A Guide for School Support Staff

Rosemary Sage

Paul Chapman
Publishing

First published 2006

 Paul Chapman Publishing
A SAGE Publications Company
1 Oliver's Yard
55 City Road
London EC1Y 1SP

SAGE Publications Inc
2455 Teller Road
Thousand Oaks, California 91320

SAGE Publications India Pvt Ltd
B-42, Panchsheel Enclave
Post Box 4109
New Dehli 110 017

Library of Congress Control Number: 2006904038

A catalogue record for this book is available from the British Library

ISBN-10 1-4129-1279-2   ISBN-13 978-1-4129-1279-2
ISBN-10 1-4129-1280-6   ISBN-13 978-1-4129-1280-8 (pbk)

Typeset by Pantek Arts Ltd, Maidstone, Kent.
Printed in Great Britain by Cromwell Press Ltd, Trowbridge, Wiltshire
Printed on paper from sustainable resources

Contents

Rosemary Sage is Senior Lecturer at the University of Leicester, heading up the learning development and support portfolio of post-graduate courses. She is a visiting professor at Nara Women's University, Japan.

Dedication

This book is dedicated to my late father, Victor Beaton. He was a wonderful communicator – able to relate to anyone and speak with a strong, resonant voice. His stories of Chico, the cheeky rabbit, who lived in the ditch surrounding our house, rivalled any of the Peter Rabbit tales! He left a lucrative career in the City to become a priest, and among his roles was that of Director of Religious Education for Suffolk. He spent time in schools and colleges, and his cheerful, utter integrity and concerned interest in others were, and still are, a constant inspiration of how life should be lived.

Preface

Increasingly, teachers and support staff have interchangeable classroom roles, and it is difficult to detect who has which! Although teachers are charged with implementing an exacting national curriculum, teaching assistants (TAs) assume responsibility for helping pupils access informal and formal learning. The roles of educators are equally important and must merge collaboratively if pupils are to achieve potential. So, communication and learning are viewed as a whole process, which is impossible to divide into parts for different professionals to pursue.

Thus, the word *educator* is used in this text for the range of adults managing learning. Teaching assistants take whole-class groups, helping to plan and implement lessons, so reference is made to whole-class, small-group and individual communication experiences as part and parcel of the school day, and anyone wanting to reflect on communication for effective learning will hopefully find it interesting.

However, as TAs focus on the teaching and learning process in detail, this book is particularly relevant to their interests, roles and concerns. They increasingly manage opportunities for specific teaching and coaching in communication, and many of the examples in this book have been explored and identified with TAs working on a Communication Opportunity Group Scheme (COGS) course, and they have also contributed to research for a new text, *COGS in the Classroom* (Sage, 2006).

Opportunities for TAs to attain recognition as professionals are increasing as their profile is raised. Part of this process for some is gaining recognition as a Higher Level Teaching Assistant (HLTA). To do this, TAs must meet published standards. This book includes activities for reflection on discussion that are related to these standards. The intention is to provide a framework within which TAs can explore ideas related to these competencies. It should be made clear that fulfilling the activities will hopefully be good preparation for TAs intending to follow the HLTA route, but will not provide a comprehensive route to meeting the standards without other input.

Exercises, extensions to tasks and other useful information can be found in the appendix section at the back of the book.

What Is Communication and Learning?

This chapter:

- introduces issues regarding communication and learning
- suggests that the leap from the informal style of home to the formal one of school is too great for children to manage successfully
- suggests that communication is taken for granted, like breathing – we do it without conscious thought
- considers evidence which points to a need to give communication more attention within learning situations

What is communication?

Communication is a complicated process that demands putting together information from many sources, and expressing thoughts with *clarity* and relevant *content*, according to established *conventions,* and an awareness of our *conduct* through the reactions of others to what we say and do. Government policies emphasise delivering the curriculum and neglect teacher understanding about how to organise talk. Cortazzi (1997) says staff and student ability to verbally express and understand each others' talk is crucial for relations. Evidence suggests that practitioners struggle. Sage et al. (2003) found in a sample of school staff that 62% felt they lacked knowledge and skills of group communication. This, of course includes teaching assistants (TAs), who are increasingly working with children who need support to communicate successfully. To provide this support, TAs need to understand what communication is and how it develops. But perhaps we should begin by asking: What is education for? How does it happen? A TA says: *Education is about thinking, communicating and learning so we can make the most of life.* A teacher states: *Education is about acquiring knowledge by working towards curriculum targets*. Does knowledge include understanding? Does your classroom role colour your views on education? Whatever your slant, you probably agree that communication is the heart of school experience.

TASK 1.1

HLTA 1.6 *Improve own practice, including through observation, evaluation and discussion with colleagues.*

Try to write your own definition of education, and then ask three colleagues to do the same. Were there any

● common points?

● references to communication?

Thinking about and discussing your thoughts on education should help you actively reflect on your practice.

We think *words* are the most important aspect of what we transmit to pupils. However, communication includes many ways of sending and receiving messages and not simply *telling things to others*. It encompasses the context in which word and non-word messages occur. For example, Luke rushes in late to class, and the teacher says: *There's a chair over there*. It is intended that the *statement* is interpreted as a *command* to sit down. Luke, however, stands puzzled until Kirn whispers: *She means sit on the chair*. The purpose and meaning of the communication is not in the words but in the context. The teacher, in full flow, wants Luke seated quickly. She assumes he can transpose between literal and non-literal information (Chomsky, 1965), but Kirn's response suggests that he needs help.

TASK 1.2

HLTA 3.2.2 *Monitor pupils' responses to learning tasks and modify the approach accordingly.*

Make a 5-minute observation of a lesson where an adult is communicating with children as they begin a session. Did you notice any examples of talk that needed to be understood at a level beyond the literal? Did the children understand? How might such situations be improved?

Many children have difficulty with inferring meaning from utterances that do not directly signal their intention and demand that the listener look beyond, behind and between them to grasp the message. The Japanese have a natural distrust of words, so adults direct children to the context and non-verbal information for understanding (Sage et al., 2004). This gives them a terrific advantage in coping with the more formal communication of school. Words frequently do not say what they mean, and you need to be an experienced communicator to understand this! Adults may say, *That's lovely*, to a child's picture, with a facial grimace suggesting otherwise!

Communication is intuitive, involving feelings, attitudes, general knowledge and social understanding. The process develops from experiences and *our impression* of a speaker. This is communicated by dress, manner, posture, voice, physical appearance and personality. The context, along with role, status, and attitudes and feelings toward the speaker, dictates whether we accept or reject the message. With regard to writing, the style of the prose and the values inherent in it engage us or fail to do so. Using communication *clearly*, with relevant *content*, according to *conventions* and *conduct* that feeds back to adjust behaviour, is the key to development.

Talking or writing, however, does not necessarily result in the receiver comprehending and assimilating information. Learning raises questions about objectives as well as views about its nature, relevance and purpose to life. Unless educators and learners relate, communicate and agree about goals and their attainment, as well as understand each other's ways of thinking and talking about them, there is little likelihood of children grasping ideas, developing abilities and conforming to educational expectations. Learning and teaching are, therefore, a communicative experience in which verbal and non-verbal information is constantly being exchanged between participants within a context that provides the meaning. Perspectives are:

1. *Components* – whereby a sender directs a message through a medium (spoken/written) to a receiver with some effect.
2. *Contexts* – whereby people create and exchange meanings in social activities which respond to the reality they experience.

Stronger emphasis is placed on the component model, but the issue is how people use communication in various situations. The component model stresses the '*what*', whereas the context one emphasises the '*how and why*' of communication. For example, the fact that you know what an egg is does not mean you can cook it. This same principle applies to communication. You may know sounds, words and sentence patterns but not be able to use them.

Do we value communication?

Not all adults are able or willing to work for continuous, cooperative endeavours with pupils, some preferring to invoke the authority of their superior knowledge or the power of their position to impose choice of instruction, whether or not learners find it helpful. While conforming pupils cope, there are others with personalities, attitudes and problems in understanding, that prevent acceptance and provoke them to rebel. Limited communication experience makes for student difficulties as well as an educator's failure to be clear, whatever the learner's competence. Sage (2000a) and Cross (2005) suggest that many behaviour problems are rooted in limited communication with poor ability to negotiate meanings. Sage and Cwenar (2003) state that adults, also, may sometimes lack communication experience in relation to children as persons and learners. Fifty per cent of teachers and 74% of support staff felt they did not have the knowledge or skill to communicate adequately with diverse groups. Teaching is not what it was when schools segregated pupils, and lessons were delivered to those with similar credentials. Now, we find children from many social, educational and cultural backgrounds, with differing abilities, interests and motivations in classes. Therefore, the language of instruction appears to be a major problem for children's learning (Sage, 2000a)

TASK 1.3

HLTA 3.3.2 Communicate effectively and sensitively with pupils to support learning.

How is your communication? Complete the profile in Appendix 1.1 to evaluate your ability. How would you seek to improve your own communication to pupils?

What are problems in classroom communication?

One of the hurdles children face is shifting from informal communicating patterns of home to the formal ones of school. Formal communication involves educators talking and pupils listening to large quantities of talk.

Sarah, age 9, says, *I can't put together what's said – too many words*. This *narrative* ability to assemble the message is generally not required in ordinary conversation, where information comes in short bursts with chances to clarify and regulate action. Importantly, in the informal situation there are equal turns among participants. This control is snatched away from children in class.

Brian, age 10, states, *I'm told off for not listening. I don't get what they're on about*. Table 1.1, therefore, summarises home and class talk to appreciate the difficulties.

Table 1.1 Characteristics of home and class talk

Home talk	Class talk
Informal, familiar style – many statements.	Formal style – many questions and commands.
Adult modifies words, sentence length, information to suit the child, signalling turn taking and a shift of topic clearly.	Language adjusted for mid-ability range – some pupils are not catered for in terms of discourse level.
Language content and context based on shared assumptions about experience. Language is particular, and more meaning is available in non-verbal ways.	Language demands frequent interpretation of non-shared assumptions. More meaning coded in words. Language is universal.
Frequent turn taking between adult and child according to social and cultural conventions.	Teacher monologue dominates. Little turn taking except within the class conventions.

Table 1.1 Continued

Home talk	Class talk
Frequent individual comments by adult and child to clarify what is shared.	Children expected to listen in silence. Teacher comments on world at large.
Generally small amounts of information shared, dependent on the context.	Large volume of information used to expand content that is not about the present context.
Ongoing checks for understanding.	Frequent reference to past information without checks for understanding.
Language is contextualised.	Language is decontextualised.
Purpose of talk is to share topics and terms of reference and to take equal turns in the dialogue. The talk normally lacks a tight focus and is unplanned.	Purpose of talk is to transmit knowledge. Talk is goal directed with emphasis on technical terms and words' meanings.
Home talk is simple in ideas and about personal concerns that involve the here and now.	Class talk is mentally complex and remote from individual concerns, referring to a context that is not normally present.
Participants' assumptions depend mainly on a specific context and can be taken for granted.	Assumptions are based on what is said in a general context and cannot be taken for granted.

What are narrative thinking and communicative competence?

A narrative framework is vital to thinking. Bruner (1990) stresses it is the '*organising principle*' of experience, knowledge and transactions within our social worlds. This does not refer just to written text, but also to *oral narratives which serve to relate personal histories, justifications, plans for the future, as well as the living narratives* experienced in family life (Wood, 1998). Sage (2000a) suggests that gaps in meaning or action during narrative events recruit the listener or reader to fill them. It is impossible to include all details and clues that are used to gather meaning. Information and opinion gap activities scaffold children's thinking, while allowing them to contribute and transform it into their own, as illustrated below.

TASK 1.4

HLTA 3.2.3 Monitor pupils' participation and progress, providing feedback to teachers, and giving constructive support to pupils as they learn.

Read this poem for youngsters and work out why many find it difficult to understand:

(Continued)

(Continued)

> *Algy met the bear.*
>
> *The bear met Algy.*
>
> *The bear was bulgy.*
>
> *The bulge was Algy.*

It does not say *the bear ate Algy*, and this gap in information has to be filled. There is a clue from the word *bulgy*. Experience of bears eating humans is used to work out the message. Narrative understanding depends on *inference* (guessing from clues), *coherence* (assembly of ideas to make meaning) and the use of *reference* (pronoun standing for a subject/object to promote fluency and rhythm, as in *Algy's a boy. He's five*).

TASK 1.5

HLTA 3.3.5 Advance pupils' learning in a range of classroom settings, including working with individuals, small groups and whole classes where the assigned teacher is not present.

Collect poems and use with a group of children to give experience of guessing the meaning by playing detective with the clues! This should develop and advance the way children engage with poetry and language.

Components of narrative

Inference, coherence and reference develop only from opportunities to use formal language, which are now rare outside classrooms because formal occasions, such as mealtimes, are in decline. They offer a chance to hear others' personal experiences as well as telling about your own. Selection and sequencing of events in a coherent way helps children shift from informal to formal communication structures. *Formal talk* is the midpoint between spoken and written communication and is an essential step in dealing with secondary modes of representation such as literacy (letters) and numeracy (numbers). Written communication is more descriptive and explicit, because events are not in present time and require assembly of context clues to grasp meaning.

Recently, communication has been included in the curriculum, as the key generic process through which human exchanges are conducted. However, Pring (2004) outlines the danger of *reductionism* (splitting a process into its parts) citing that the use of the word '*skill*' to describe *communication,* results in discrete teaching approaches such as vocabulary, sounds, etc. Skills are involved in communication, such as maintaining eye contact, projecting voice, using hands demonstrably, choosing the correct medium and presenting arguments to different audiences. These techniques are learnt and perfected through coaching and practice. Sage (2003) argues, however, that *communication is much more than skills*, and that it is a cognitive *process* requiring the understanding of audiences and situations as well as knowing what to say and do appropriately. The pursuit of skills must not be an end in itself. This relationship between thinking and communicating is not properly understood in learning and rarely addressed successfully in schools (Sage, 2004).

Narrative thinking connects to communicative competence because social interaction and cultural practices in shaping human development are stressed (Wood, 1998: 50). Verbal interactions are 'formative', as talking to and with others exposes us to communicative functions. Listening to and telling narratives monitors communication use, taking account of listener perspectives and planning coherent and comprehensible speech sequences (Wood, 1998: 159). Therefore, the sort of communication practices children experience are crucial to narrative thinking and communicative competence.

TASK 1.6

HLTA 3.3.3 Promote and support the inclusion of all pupils in the learning activities in which you are involved.

Carry out a 10-minute observation of a whole-class teaching session, scoring when adults talk and when children talk. What is the proportion of adult-to-pupil talk? How could pupil talk be increased? For instance, have you seen pupils encouraged to use talk partners, or act out experience in circle time?

What are the implications for communicative competence?

Although communicative competence is essential and predictive of school success (Brigman et al., 1999), there are challenges when adjusting from informal home relationships to formal school ones (Hargreaves, 1997). Brigman et al. identified the essentials. These are the *applied learning abilities* of listening, attending, following directions, and problem solving, together with the *social abilities* such as working, playing cooperatively and forming as well as maintaining relationships. Successful exchanges need both support and instruction to develop effectively and cannot be left to chance (Sage, 2000a).

However, school may be less intellectually and linguistically demanding than home (Tizard and Hughes, 1984). In class, the initiation-response-feedback (IRF) pattern is common in adult–child exchanges. This involves children listening for longer and answering questions away from their meaningful contexts. Moreover, learning varies between cultures, with children of certain cultures advantaged in school because adults ask them instructive questions, while others are not so questioned because this is not part of home practice.

Have standards of communicative competence declined?

Concerns have been raised about children's communication competence on entering and leaving school. Studies suggest deficits in preschool abilities (Bell,

1991; Boyer, 1992; Lees et al., 2001; Sage, 2002). At the other end of the age spectrum, employers identify communication as a weak ability in the workforce (Hogarth et al., 2001). Current initiatives attempt to develop key abilities, such as communication for learners aged 16–19 in England (Hayward and Fernandez, 2004). The decline of manufacturing over 30 years and the growth of people-services, such as tourism, have shifted the workforce profile. Blue-collar jobs, requiring physical and craft skills, have declined from 51% to 38%, while white-collar work, demanding interpersonal and communication abilities, has increased from 27% to 41% (Hayward and Fernandez, 2004).

These changes affect the experiences and competences of children. The changes include the effects of television and computers, earlier nursery attendance because of more working mothers, the shift toward informal eating, increased parental break-ups, less family support, and greater job mobility. Views of child qualities and abilities have also altered, with an earlier formalised curriculum and expectations of age competences. The result is greater criticism of child achievement at Foundation Stage 1. The political notion of 'value added' explains increased attention to preschool education from 1996. The ability to cooperate, attend, listen, and express ideas creatively, critically and coherently is important if the ideal of confident 'lifelong learners' is to be realised. The views of Baljit, a Year 1 pupil, focus on the importance of communication for learning.

What I think of school, by Baljit (Year 1 pupil)

Hi! I'm Baljit. Friends call me Bob. Miss says my nickname's right. I bob about all the time. I'm never still! I'm not good at work. I was five in August. I do Year 1 objectives. It's not fair. Bola's two weeks younger. She does reception ones. She was longer in nursery than me. I'm behind. Mum wants me to be like Sadeeda – sitting quietly and writing. To help, we started a Family Numeracy Project. Mum had lessons. She liked them. The teachers made her feel good. I took part in COGS (The Communication Opportunity Group Scheme). It helped me think and speak. Learning is better now. I went two times a week for ten weeks – for half an hour.

[Later, Baljit was asked what happened at COGS.]

There were seven others. I liked it. We did lots of talking. We never got told we were wrong. We learnt the 'Algy and the Bear' poem. I said 'bulgy' meant really big. The bear had eaten Algy. It didn't say so. You had to work it out. We made sentences in games. We brought our own things to talk about. It was easy to listen. Teachers showed ways to say things. We said what we were feeling. We moved around and had fun.

We practised speaking clearly and looking at each other, so others heard and thought about what we said. We had games with objects. We took one from a box when the music stopped. We had to say what we liked about it. It got easy. We learnt about rules. We learnt to think about others. We learnt how bodies help send messages. The way we answer questions gives a good or bad view of us. The others in the group told us what we did well. Teachers helped us be better – to speak more clearly by making words louder or slower. The teachers thought we would understand this if we told each other. We had to mark each other and talk about how to do it. I liked this. We finished the group last week. I was sorry. We did things together. COGS is better than class. It helps me learn better.

COGS rationale

The teaching strategy discussed in Baljit's case study is embedded in the COGS philosophy and developed by Sage (1986) in response to pupil underachievement in literacy and numeracy, when tests provided no answers. Children were asked to perform at a higher level in literacy and numeracy than achieved orally where there was difficulty in comprehending the gist of a narrative and expressing ideas coherently.

COGS facilitates the development and expression of ideas verbally and non-verbally, by developing narrative thinking and communicative competence over 14 goals. These are adapted for children as young as four years up to post-graduate level. Goals are not designed to be applicable to specific ages but use the child's or adult's zone of 'proximal' Vygotsky (1962) or 'potential' development (ZPD), (Alexander, 2003). Table 1.2 demonstrates narrative thinking progression in the first seven goals, which are extended from eight to 14 in more complex tasks. Ideas are developed within principles of clarity, content, convention and conduct.

Table 1.2 Progression of ideas in the COGS framework

Goal	Idea development	Description
1	Record	Produce a range of ideas
2	Recite	Group simple ideas
3	Refer	Compare ideas
4	Replay	Sequence ideas in time
5	Recount	Explain ideas –Why? How?
6	Report	Introduce, discuss, describe, evaluate ideas
7	Relate	Setting, events, actions, results, reactions

There are five tasks at each goal level – four oral and one creative writing – the ratio found in life. Tasks target specific and core communication competences common to all acts. Games relax and support specific development in a circle format that facilitates interaction. A 'tell, show, do and coach' approach, including systematic sequencing of teaching with review, demonstration, guided practice and corrective, supportive feedback, proved to be most effective (Wang et al., 1994). In order to share meanings through talk, there is a mixture of group and independent activity, so enacting Vygotsky's (1962) notion that *what the child can do in co-operation today he can do alone tomorrow*. The COGS is compatible with Alexander's (2003) dialogic teaching with the needed conditions. Firstly, the setting is collective, with teacher and pupils addressing learning together. Secondly, it is reciprocal, as both listen to each other. Thirdly, it is cumulative, with pupils **and** teachers building on ideas, chaining them into coherent lines of enquiry. Finally, the atmosphere supports, helping all speak freely, without fear or embarrassment.

COGS principles highlight the following:

- communication that is message orientated
- learning that is both active and interactive
- activities that are learner-centred and controlled
- empathy and cooperation, valuing feelings, feedback and mutual support
- the educator role as proactive facilitator and modeller (Sage, 2000a).

COGS enables a cooperative atmosphere in which children have relative freedom and can take risks with ideas. They trust and empathise with each other and take part in peer review. Baljit experienced COGS as a halfway house between home and school. Relationships are formal and rule-bound but with many opportunities to co-construct understanding of what is happening and what is being learnt with peers and teachers.

In literacy and numeracy hours, Baljit had difficulty in listening to teacher-talk. When the class read the 'Big Book', he found it hard to concentrate. In both lessons, he responded either in a whisper, inadequately or inaccurately when pressured to answer closed questions. He was not alone, with only two out of 34 in class responding appropriately. Even they felt the need to be right, as one was admonished for inaccuracy: *Colin, you counted wrongly. Can you believe a boy getting a 2A in SATS can't count out pencils for the class?*

Attention in the numeracy lesson improved when Baljit was set a problem to order four differently shaped and sized plastic beakers, according to how much liquid they could hold. This allowed children to move to the water table. Baljit understood immediately how to solve this, leading discussion with a clear voice. Later, when pupils were asked what else could measure water, he answered brightly, *'a jug, a glass'*. The response, *That's right*, was the only praise given. Despite this success, the educators appeared not to value practical activities. When questioned about doing *writing*, they said: *We'll do proper work tomorrow*, suggesting that writing was work but not speaking was so defined.

To summarise, Baljit was passive in literacy and numeracy, because he thrives only in active situations when he can interact and problem solve. Transmitted information, as if the mind is a blank slate, gave scant opportunity to co-construct ideas with others, so he frequently lost the narrative thread and became inattentive and sometimes disruptive in class.

TASK 1.7

HLTA 2.9 Know a range of strategies to establish a purposeful learning environment and to promote good behaviour.

Keep a reflective journal of a child who presents as inattentive and disruptive. Are communication problems at the root of this behaviour? Suggest strategies for improving communication so that attention and motivation can be improved.

What are learning obstacles?

Specific obstacles

Some learning obstacles are specific to Baljit, but others affect all. Browne (2004) states that *ethnicity, poverty and season of birth, rather than gender* have most impact on progress. Research on male–female brain differences seems inconclusive.

So, gender aside, pupils may be adversely affected by an August birth with less schooling than older Year 1 peers. Bilingualism is another factor. Baljit's mother tongue is Gujarati, but English is used for education. Bilingualism is advantageous if concepts have developed in the mother tongue, and when this is maintained, children have deeper language knowledge and understanding than monolinguals, because of skill transference (Cummins, 2003). However, if school does not value the mother tongue (as with Baljit), negative cognitive and emotional effects result. Firstly, productive use is lost within two years of school (Thompson, 1999). Secondly, children lack confidence to participate (Parke and Drury, 2002). With Baljit, speech diffidence was apparent, as was inability to follow class talk. He was capable but underachieving, and this was attributed to lack of effort rather than communication problems.

General obstacles

Obstacles affecting all pupils include an abstract, meaningless, overly academic and over-assessed, discontinuous curriculum, alongside limited awareness of ways to promote communication. With academic abilities prioritised over personal, the value of cooperative ways of working is overlooked. Moreover, such policies emphasise long blocks of directed class teaching, giving play and active learning low status.

The Desirable Outcomes for Children's Learning (QCAA, 1996) barely feature play, with goals and guidance contradicting research. Although early learning goals include reference to play, the focus is on *what* children should learn rather than *how* (Miller, 2001).

The National Literacy Strategy (NLS) supports interactive teaching, but whether pupil contributions are encouraged, expected and extended is questionable. English et al. (2002) note tension between NLS advice that teaching should be both interactive and well paced. Hardman et al. (2003) found that it encourages *more directive forms of teaching with little opportunities for pupils to explore and elaborate on their ideas.* Burns and Myhill (2004) affirm that *teacher led questioning and explanation still dominates,* as do teachers' objectives. *Interaction as participation was differentially experienced by higher and lower ability boys and girls, with few opportunities for pupil initiation or extended response.*

This contrasts with the target-driven Key Stage 1 curriculum in the NLS (QCA, 1999, 2000) and repackaged speaking and listening objectives (QCA, 2003a). Termly objectives assume that pupils develop in similar ways and rates with no space to accommodate individual differences. The early learning goal title includes communication with language and literacy, implying a holistic approach compared with the Key Stage 1 reductive focus on parts. However, oracy and literacy are separately documented, so it is unsurprising that the shift between them is not understood.

Baljit's class experienced an unvarying form of initiation-response-feedback (IRF) patterns between teacher and pupils, so limiting risk taking, narrative thinking and the sharing of meanings. Teaching promoted closed questions and one-word answers, evaluated for correctness. Closed questions help pupils perform better on factual tests, but achievement is higher when children encounter demanding, open-ended questions, where they speculate, hypothesise and discuss more. Alexander's (2004) dialogic teaching, where adults and pupils are in conversation with each other, builds on this knowledge.

As pointed out at the outset of this chapter, communication is a complicated process that involves skills in and appreciation of *clarity, content, conventions* and *conduct.* It is vital that TAs develop their own knowledge of communication, and also strategies to support the development of communication for the children they support.

Key Points

- Communication and relationships are basic to learning.
- Communication involves more than words, and non-verbal aspects are crucial to grasping meaning.
- Evidence indicates that children enter school lacking experience in formal communication and the means to learn.
- Research suggests that educators lack sufficient knowledge and ability in communication theory and practice to support learning.
- Teaching communication, as in COGS, has a huge impact on learning and behaviour.
- Educators with a role to help pupils access learning must develop knowledge and skills in cognition and communication to help children achieve.

2

How Do Communication and Learning Develop?

This chapter:

- confirms that communication occurs through interaction with others from the time a child is born
- traces the development of communication, from cries for attention to speech babbles, which become words when linked to referents such as people, objects and actions
- shows how the above skills enable the building of sentence patterns and allow understanding and expression of feelings, intentions and views in a clear, coherent way
- confirms that communication development proceeds alongside brain and body growth
- considers the role of the educator in the development of communication

Brain growth

Brain development has been less considered than that of the body because it is not so easily seen, but its aspects can be viewed below, showing its role in processing input and organising output. A table of development is given in Appendix 2.1 providing a context for understanding physical, mental, social and emotional development.

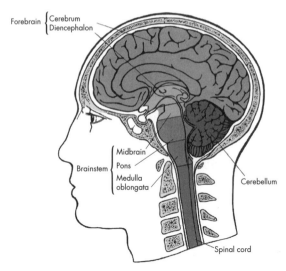

Figure 2.1 Shows the brain and spinal cord with various parts.

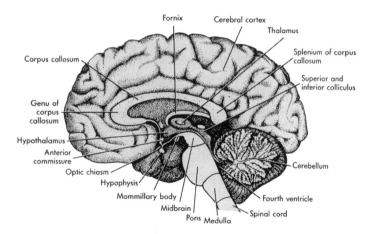

Figure 2.2 Presents a brain section showing relationships of cerebral cortex (*cognition*), cerebellum (*motor control*), thalamus (*input and output relay*) and brainstem (*ears and eyes, bladder and breath control*) that regulate body functions.

TASK 2.1

HLTA 2.5 Know the key factors that can affect the way pupils learn.

What aspects of brain development do you think are ignored in present policies and practices to teach literacy? (see Appendix 2.1).

In line with brain development is the development of communication, which we need to understand in order to assess the use of this in school.

Before words; first words and words together

Before words

Let me introduce you to my daughter, Helen. She slipped into the world with a lusty cry – a series of pulses with a vowel-like quality lasting around a second and punctuated by a brief pause to take in air. There was much to feel, smell, taste, see and, above all, hear. First needs were very basic – to be warm, fed, sheltered and protected, and I quickly differentiated Helen's cries for hunger (*loud, rhythmic and persistent*), pain (*tenser with high pitches and jumps*), discomfort (*distressing whimper, only half a second in length, in shorter sequences*), etc. These cries brought about a response, so establishing the basic requirement of communication – a trusting, caring relationship – as well as exercising the vocal chords and opening the lungs in preparation for learning sounds, words and sentences.

Helen's eyes were tightly shut for her first few minutes of life outside her cosy cot inside me, but during that time she heard:

- over 100 utterances (e.g. *Its a girl. Shes gorgeous – just like her mum!*)
- over 500 words with over 2,000 vowels and consonants.

Once Helen had stopped crying, there was no way she could shut these sounds out apart from falling asleep, which came later. That is the peculiar power of sound. You cannot shut your ears as you can your eyes! Helen was born into an English-speaking community and needed to learn the following:

- 20 vowels (*a, e, i, o, u* and their combinations) and 24 consonants
- 300 ways of combining sounds into sequences ($s+t+r+i+ng$ = string)
- vocabulary of at least 50,000 words
- ability to understand words of others (100,000 words plus)
- 1,000 rules of grammar to make acceptable sentences
- voice dynamics (pitch, pace, pause, power, pronunciation) with facial expressions and gestures to give words different meanings according to situation
- ability to understand social rules, to know what to say, how and when!

All this is for the future. At the initial stage, apart from Helen's basic cries to have her needs supplied, there were biological noises such as cooing, gurgling, coughing and spluttering, sucking, burping and being sick! After 16 weeks, the cooing faded to be replaced by more definite and controlled sounds in babbling chains (dadadadada, abaabaabaaba, etc.) I copied these back, setting up a routine like a dance. These melodies and rhythms are the prelude to words.

Until this stage, children from different language backgrounds sound the same, but now they begin to show differences. An English child utters in a tum-ti-tum rhythm, in contrast to a French one, who displays more of a rat-tat-tat. A Chinese child sounds sing-song and youngsters who are deaf will present as increasingly abnormal with their utterances lacking melodic and rhythmical variations.

At about a year, we hear the final stage in the pre-speech sequence – short utterances of 1–2 syllables long with a regular, predictable melody and rhythm – called the proto-word (Crystal, 1994). No one was certain what Helen's first utterance meant. It sounded like *Daddy*, but this interpretation did not always fit the situation. It was meaningful when said while pointing to Dad coming back from work, but not when uttered randomly while in the bath when he was absent. In the transition from pre-language to language proper, children produce proto-words in which the sounds are clear, but the meaning is not. Only when the sound of an utterance and its meaning both become obvious do we have the final step – the first proper word!

First words

Much sound-making precedes the first word, but there is a greater amount of sound-receiving. When do children start to understand the speech that adults direct to them? The baby soon interprets tone of voice, facial expression and body language. She waves bye-bye long before being able to say the words, and responds to *No* by stopping an undesirable activity because of the power given to utterance when accompanied by a stern expression. These responses to non-verbal signs are the first step to understanding words. At 2–4 months, contrasts in meaning come to be appreciated – the difference between soothing, playful or angry voices is discerned. At 6–9 months a child recognises the different use of certain utterances in specific situations. *Bye-bye* produces a wave and *Clap hands* brings both hands together! Many children will understand more than 20 words before their first year, and the understanding of the link between a word and its referent – object, place or action – together with the ability to articulate a combination of consonants and vowels, heralds the first words.

Words together

We probably think that a conversation is impossible without words, but look at the interaction between Helen and myself when she was one week old.

Helen: (persistent loud crying).

Me: Oh dear! What a noise. Isn't anyone paying you attention? (*picks up Helen*).

Helen: (crying drops to a softer sob).

Me: Let's see what's the matter (*looks inside the nappy*). No problem there. I think you're hungry.

Helen: (spluttering noises).

Me: (*whips out a boob!*) Here's some nice, warm milk. Yummy, yummy!

Helen: (nuzzling, sucking noises).

Me: Just what the doctor ordered. Milk in two convenient packs, eh!

No other human interaction is like this! It may seem odd to talk to someone who does not understand, but the point is to communicate and form a relationship from the word *Go*. Almost everything a mother says is controlled by what the baby does and the noises it makes. All the yawns, burps, sneezes, splutters, coos, etc., are interpreted as messages of huge significance. Baby makes a noise and mother produces one in return, introducing extra melodies, rhythms, voice tones, movements, facial expressions and gestures into the exchange to see the reaction. The baby responds accordingly, and there is great satisfaction all round! The foundation for social interaction is laid, and the framework in which words are introduced allows communication to become more meaningful and mentally challenging.

This dialogue diminishes when the child enters school, as the pattern is adult monologue, with pupils listening and answering the odd question to check that facts are understood. It is important to note that children may have adequate speech and language structure for informal exchanges, but be unable to use it for effective communication, thinking, social interaction and personal control in more formal contexts. In schools, spoken and written words are the important medium.

TASK 2.2

HLTA 2.5 Know the key factors that can affect the way pupils learn.

Consider this conversation between a teaching assistant (TA) and 6-year-old Anna.

TA: (reinforcing a previous lesson on conservation with Anna, a child with a hearing problem). Anna, hold these lumps and tell me whether there's the same amount in each.

Anna: I think so...

TA: Watch, I'm changing one of the round ones into a long shape like a sausage roll. (*Shapes one of the balls into a sausage shape in front of Anna*). Is there the same amount in both lumps?

Anna: (*Nods her head*).

TA: If you put it back into the lump, it would be the same.

Anna: Would be the same. (**imitation**).

TA: It would be the same but longer and thinner, but, as I haven't put in any more or taken any away, it must be the same amount (**reinforcement**).

Anna: It's different (shape) but same stuff.

TA: The lump is larger around but shorter than the sausage, which is longer and thinner. They are **different** in **shape** but not in **amount** (**expansion**).

(Continued)

(Continued)

Did you notice the following patterns in the previous exchange?

1. **Expansions:** *the adult repeats what the child has just said, expanding it into a complete grammatical sentence.*

2. **Imitations:** *the child imitates what the adult has just said either exactly or simplified so that it is less complex.*

3. **Reinforcement:** *responses by the adult to the form of the child's answer.*

During conversations, adults not only give children information, but also help them *structure ideas* through words. Language is, therefore, central to human experience, being a key vehicle for thought and social contact. Humans are mutually dependent, and effective communication between them requires that they:

- know the forms of language they share; how words sound, combine and are arranged in sentences (competence in phonology, grammar and syntax)
- can bring together verbal and non-verbal messages to understand the communication of others, and use both modes to convey their own meaning (competence in information processing and production, plus semantics)
- understand and use the conventions that determine how people communicate with each other and appreciate each other's intention (competence in pragmatics)
- can vary their style (register) of communication to suit the needs of different listeners and understand that used by others in both dialogues (short exchanges) and monologues (long narratives) (competence in conversation moves and narrative thinking)
- understand how language- and communication-use varies within different social contexts (competence in sociolinguistics).

Issues about communication

Children may have problems mastering these areas of competence, some of which are linguistic, and others cognitive and social. Often difficulties are not detected, because we are ineffective communicators with limited understanding of this complex process. Thus, if children function adequately in short dialogues, we assume that they can do so in the monologue situations of a classroom, where adults talk for most of the time and pupils have to assemble chunks of information from a variety of sources, to make meaning. That many children struggle should come as no surprise, when we appreciate the leap they have to make between short and long exchanges.

Traditionally, attention has been given to three types of competence – phonology (*sound system*); grammar (*word functions: nouns, verbs, etc.*) and syntax, (*word arrangements: subject–verb–object plus phrase and clause structure*). Appendix 4.1 provides information on language features. This emphasis on language diverts attention away from narrative structure and how meaning is conveyed. Educators quickly pick up distorted sounds and limited vocabulary, but narrative problems are put down to poor listening. Levels of sentence processing illustrate this. For example: *The dog is in the entrance*. The sentence conveys little on its own and has meaning only within a specific context. The dog in the entrance may be real or representational, and may be there waiting for something or entering/exiting the place. Reference to context and ability to use experience, knowledge and clues to refer, infer and cohere the meaning are the mental operations that integrate with linguistic knowledge to produce communication. The context is essential to understanding the nature of the whole, and general knowledge of doggy behaviour suggests they have a penchant for diving down earthy openings, sometimes getting stuck and not returning! Language structure thus merges with narrative structure to achieve meaning. It is clear that putting together monologues is impossible without a well-developed ability to analyse, synthesise and evaluate information – skills that are weak in both children and adults, because of a lack of opportunities to develop talking and thinking in our modern, hurried lives (Sage, 2000b)(Table 2.1).

Table 2.1

	Stage	What is processed
1	Sound processing	sound wave transmitted into a neural spectrum
2	Extraction of phonetic features	voice, friction, nasality, etc.
3	Analysis of the sound sequence	consonant–vowel patterns
4	Recognition of the sound sequence	the series of six words
5	Association of words with sound, sight, feeling images	dog – wiry, furry, barks
6	Recognition of the word structure	*subject* (noun phrase: *the dog*; verb: *is*; object: *in the entrance* (object phrase)
7	Representation of the proposition (probably in pictorial form)	theme – dog located in the entrance of a rabbit hole
8	Mental operation to infer and evaluate the information	working out why the dog is in the entrance as a step toward understanding
9	Interpretation of the meaning from context clues and general knowledge	bringing together available information from the context for understanding. In this case, the dog is in the entrance to a rabbit hole, and only his rump is visible – he's hard on the trail of some scared bunnies!

Pupils experience communication problems because they have undeveloped higher thinking processes, and the conventions of communication-use at home are different from those of school. At home, it is children who talk and question, but in school, the process reverses. Unless experienced in the variety of social rules that operate in different contexts, children will find school communication a hindrance rather than a help to learning.

Why is communication more important than language?

Communicative competence is more important than linguistic competence in terms of making relationships and understanding what is going on. Mary, age 8, illustrates this. Her TA asks whether she is going on the school trip to the Space Centre, but Mary replies with a statement about Mum's recent spell in hospital. Sentences are produced with accurate pronunciation, syntax and intonation, but she never looks at the speaker, and she talks at length, but often without relevance to the context. The school regards Mary as a poor listener, but she displays a higher-order problem in communication. This performance would be acceptable for a 3-year-old, but not for a midprimary pupil:

> **TA**: *Mary, are you going to the Space Centre on Friday?*

> **M**: *Mum's in hospital. She's had an operation. I see her from school. Gramps picks me up. We get Nan and we're off. We have an Indian after. Dad sees Mum later.*

How do children develop language?

Some theories of language development are worth examining, as support strategies are based on them.

Imitation

According to the theory of imitation, language results from imitation of adults. However, a childs language is unique and creative from the beginning, reducing more of what is heard than straight imitating. Since much language heard is imperfect, imitation theory cannot be a complete explanation.

Reinforcement

Another theory holds that children are shaped into language by reinforcement patterns. Although this applies to aspects such as pronunciation, when an adult models a word for repetition, there is no evidence that it is systematically applied to all grammar learning.

Analysis

The theory of analysis emphasises the ability to analyse adult language patterns, and extract rules from them, which children copy and simplify for their own use. There is truth in this, because when you tell children a story to be retold, they do so in a simplified way to match thinking and language levels. Such analyses, however, are well beyond infants.

Language acquisition device

Another theory holds that children are born to sort and learn rules for language *transformations*. Chomsky (1965) proposed that sentences have an essential meaning (deep structure) that is transformed by rules into a specific sentence (surface structure). If the deep structure is *Mark likes pears*, transformational rules can turn this into an active question, *Does Mark like pears?*, or a passive one, *Are pears liked by Mark?*, and so on. This is complex, but it makes sense that children have some system for dealing with language heard.

No single alternative provides a comprehensive theory of language development, accounting for all that is observed, or dealing adequately with word meaning. There is agreement, however, that there is a biological underpinning to language-learning and a structure for sound and sentence development, as outlined below.

Development of the sound system of English

At **0–1 year**, we have the first words with much individual variation, and then development proceeds as shown in Table 2.2.

Table 2.2

Lip	Tongue (front)	Tongue (back)
1–2 years: *p b m w*	*t d n*	
2–2.5 years: *p b m w*	*t d n*	*k g ng h*
2.5–3.5 years: *p b m w f*	*t d n s y l*	*k g ng h*
3.5–4.5 years: *p b m f w v*	*t d n s y l z*	*k g ng h sh ch j*
4.5 + years: *p b m t v w*	*t d n s z l r th y*	*k g ng h sh ch j*
5–6 years: *th*	*r*	
6–7 years: blends: *tw tr dr pl str shr spl*		

Some children have not acquired the sound system by 7 years, leading to problems in acquiring word-building skills for reading and spelling.

Development of word patterns (syntax)

Table 2.3

Age in years	Feature	Example
1–2	Two-word combinations No sense of word order	*doggy nice* *biky want*
2–3	Three-word combinations Talk about the present only	*He lose sock* *Where daddy go?* *Give mummy book*
3–4	Four-word combinations Use of statements, questions, comments Associate ideas: (knife and fork) Many words left out in a sequence	*Dan kicking ball there*
4–5	Uses coordinating words (*and*, *but*, *so*) and connectives (*because*, *where*) Uses five attributes to describe (shape, name, colour, size, feel, etc.)	*I like nuts but I don't* *like peas.* *Square brick. It's red, big* *and hard*
5–6	Uses language beyond the immediate situation. Orders ideas in some way	**Q.** *If baby cries, what* *does Mummy do?* **A.** *She picks him up and* *investigates what's wrong*
6–8	Tells back information with half the details correct. Uses features to connect up talk: *then*, *after*, *before*, *however* Replays events in the past – a holiday or weekend	

TASK 2.3

HLTA 3.2.1 Be able to support teachers in evaluating pupils' progress through a range of assessment activities.

Choose a child that you know in the 1–8 years range and carry out an observation in a context where they can speak without too many restraints – an informal and/or play situation. Do they match up with the language guidelines?

What needs to be checked to assess whether a child can follow a lesson?

The previous section has introduced a developmental structure for sound and sentence formation, but acquisition does not mean that a child can use it. To cope with the amount of talk that happens in school, a child must have the following conversational moves in place (Sage, 2000b).

Checklist of conversation moves – can the pupil:

1. answer a *closed* what, who, when, where question demanding a specific response?
2. contribute an idea (even if not entirely appropriate) showing *turn taking* ability
3. listen and respond, showing *maintenance* moves such as eye contact for 75% of the time, smiling, nodding, etc.?
4. answer an *open* how or why question demanding an explanation?
5. initiate a new idea in dialogue that fits with the topic?

If all moves are in place, this indicates an ability to follow spoken or written narratives. Listening (move 3) with forward posture and maintained eye contact suggests concentration and cooperation in exchanges. If attention wanders, it is a sign that the listener is bored or finds the information presented in an unhelpful way or above discourse level. Answering open questions (move 4) demands ability to express cause and effect and link events. *Baljit, why are you drinking milk? Because I like it better than orange.* This is the base for putting together information. Initiating a new idea (move 5) shows ability to connect ideas logically within the theme. It demands an overview of the situation and an understanding of the parts that fit together to make a whole (top-down and bottom-up processing).

Do not assume that children have these moves on starting school. Many secondary pupils have problems with *why* and *how* questions and cannot follow the lesson narrative easily, make explanations or give instructions. Skills and Enterprise Briefings (Mason, 1996) suggest that communication is the weakest ability in the workplace. Research suggests that even talented and gifted pupils have difficulties with narrative structure, as confirmed by Wilde (2003) from her work with this population on the COGS.

TASK 2.4

HLTA 3.2.2 Monitor pupils' responses to learning tasks and modify their approach accordingly.

Take any pupil and check their communication competence against the five conversational moves.

Comment

The rate of language and communication development differs from one child to the next, and many in secondary schools communicate only at the 5-year level (Sage, 2004). They chat but have problems following the connected discourse of instruction and explanation and making a coherent response. Language development has occurred, but narrative thinking has fallen behind, probably because of restricted opportunities to use language in a variety of ways. Narrative also has a developmental structure (Sage, 2000a).

Narrative structure

record	produce ideas
recite	arrange ideas in a limited way, but not in a time sequence
refer	compare ideas
replay	sequence ideas in time
recount	explain ideas (*Why? How?*)
report	discuss ideas, giving an opinion
relate	tell a story with setting, events, actions, reactions

This is a guide to how we develop our ability to deal with a number of ideas, and it is not difficult to understand the close relation between narrative ability and thinking. Bruner (1966) suggests that language and thought are separate until age 6. They then come together as an aid to memory, problem solving and analysis. Dale (1976) says mastering the linguistic system is not the same thing as putting it to work. Language is not used for many functions – memory, classification, and inner speech – until a point in development considerably later than the mastery of structure. Putting language to work is what developing narrative is about, but school puts a brake on talk and does not easily facilitate development of thinking and expression.

How can you help facilitate communication development?

Use the guides to sound, sentence and narrative structure to work out where your pupil/s fall on the developmental continuum. Try to encourage the level above by modelling this yourself so children hear the structures, but do not pressure them to achieve these until they respond freely. For example: *sounds* – if these are at the 5-year stage but not yet reaching the 6-year level, pronouncing *th* and *r* correctly, use words with these sounds, giving opportunity to hear them, but do not require repetition until this happens spontaneously. Similarly, with *sentences* – if children are using language to talk about the past and future, they should be encouraged to hear stories and tell them back. With regard to *narrative*, see whether a child can express a number of things about an object. For example, *a cup: It's white, round, with a curly handle, blue stripes around the top, made of china, with a name on the bottom and a chip on the rim*, etc. This is the beginning of narrative expression, as once children can generate ideas they will start to arrange them to make them clear. See where they are developmentally, and stimulate the next level by modelling.

Of course, development does not just happen in one aspect only. Emotional progress happens alongside physical and mental growth, and it is important to understand the stages in which they occur, as they arise out of communicative experiences, which, when negative, stunt maturation.

Emotional development

> *Life is a comedy for those who think and a tragedy for those who feel.*
> *(Horace Walpole)*

Mr Biggs was telling Mark off for kicking Kirn in the playground. Mark responded angrily by shouting, *I dont care*, his eyes filling with tears.

Mark shows by tears that he is sad, even if his head is saying words to the contrary. These two minds, the emotional and the rational, operate in tight harmony for the most part. Feelings are essential to thought and vice versa. When passions surge, however, the balance tips, and the emotional mind takes the upper hand, the cortex deferring to the limbic system. Connections between the limbic structures (thalamus, hypothalamus, basal ganglia and amygdala) and the cerebral cortex, through the amygdala (almond-shaped part in the midbrain), strike a balance between head and heart, thought and feeling. An important aspect of learning is learning how to deal with your emotions.

Of concern to teachers is the child's aggression and attachment (dependency). The earliest patterns of interactions between carer and infant seem to be a kind of *dance,* as we saw in the case of Helen, in which the child signals with eye contact, smiles and chuckles and the adult responds. Attachment to the child may be affected by the ability of the pair to achieve satisfactory communication with one another. Communication, therefore, is an essential base for emotional development, and researchers have looked at the connection between this and behaviour (Cohen, 1996).

There are sequences in the development of attachments going from diffuse to single and then multiple attachments (Ainsworth, 1973). In older children, there is a shift away from dependent behaviours, such as clinging, holding and touching, toward mature forms such as seeking attention and approval. Children differ in the strength and quality of their early attachments and the speed in which they pass from immature to mature forms of dependency. Consistency in dependent behaviour is more notable in females than males, and this is the reason why there are more boys in school with emotional and behaviour problems. Individual differences are partly determined by care practices, although the child's temperament may be influential. Among older children, the degree of dependency seems to be jointly determined by the amount of reward and punishment that adults provide in response to the child's bids for dependency.

Trends in aggressive behaviour are less clear than for attachment, but it is suggested that there is a shift from physical to verbal aggression, as the child gets older (Goodenough, 1931). Individual differences appear marked, with boys showing more physical aggression, probably because of their strength and hormones, at all ages. Consistency in aggression through life is more apparent in males than females. There is reason to suppose that the baby comes equipped with a link between frustration and aggression, as this is such a common response in all children. Other responses to frustration can be learnt. Some child-rearing practices have been consistently linked with high levels of aggression, and these include rejection, high levels of physical punishment, and a combination of permissiveness and punishment. The context for emotional development is vital, and Erikson (1963) highlights this in stages of emotional maturity based on contrasts.

Erikson's stages of maturity

1. early infancy: trust versus mistrust
2. late infancy: autonomy versus shame and doubt
3. early childhood: initiative versus guilt
4. middle childhood: competence versus inferiority
5. adolescence: identity versus role confusion
6. early adulthood: intimacy versus isolation
7. late adulthood: self-acceptance versus despair.

As the child, adolescent, and younger and older adult experience life, they develop positive or negative concepts of themselves in relation to what is communicated to them. For example, if infants set up good communicative relationships with others, they will learn *trust*, but if these relationships are bad, *mistrust* occurs. Erikson proposes a growth pattern of constructs, which slot into other learning. When in school and able to compare performance with others, the child grasps an idea of his competence in relation to them. If he sees himself doing worse than peers, feelings of inferiority will be experienced and learnt. Sage (2003) argues that these abstract concepts, based on fundamental notions of good and bad, are the way a child analyses the world. All early experience, such as feeding and care, generate, good or bad feelings for the child. These become the base measure for judging succeeding events.

Clearly, the concept of self that emerges from experiences includes both the childs view of herself (self concept); her body and abilities (self-image) and her degree of self-esteem (value for self). The earliest stage is the discovery that she is separate from others, constant and continuous. By the age of 2 years the child has learnt her name and by 3 has achieved a measure of autonomy as a result of developing physical, mental, social and emotional abilities. At 4 years, the child is possessive about space and things, but by 6 can verbalise thoughts and emotions, forming positive or negative judgements.

Meadows (1993) reminds us, however, that children cannot be relied on to accurately express their feelings, as it takes years to identify and communicate these. Many children also appear to have problems with communicating effectively in formal contexts. Children with low self-esteem are anxious and have more difficulties coping with school. Those with high self-esteem have achievements valued and praised, experiencing a warm relationship with clear communication and limits set on behaviour (Merry, 1998).

How can we support emotional and communication development?

Terms like *emotional literacy* demonstrate the importance of attending to feelings. Research on emotional development and self-concept suggests that the communicative relationship between the child and others is the key to successful learning. In our relationships with others, we learn what they think of us, and even if this is not communicated in words, it will be in actions such as tone of voice, facial expressions and gestures. Wragg (1994) reminds us that in schools, four out of five comments to children are negative, so we can make an effort to reverse this and give feedback that is largely positive.

TASK 2.5

HLTA 3.3.2 Communicate effectively and sensitively with pupils to support their learning.

Make an audit of adult responses to children within a lesson context. You could tally these, or tape and transcribe a portion of the lesson for analysis later. Analyse these to ascertain the ratio of positive to negative comments. Suggest ways to turn negative comments into positive ones.

Social development and schools

No man is an island, entire of itself (John Donne)

Children are born into a society and need to learn to socialise. To do this successfully within norms is a major task for any child. Five theories are reference points for our attitudes and views.

The ethological theory (Bowlby, 1969)

This targets inborn, instinctive patterns of interaction. The child provokes care by cries and movements, and prolongs it with smiles and chuckles. With development, instinctive patterns come under the child's control. Attention is focused on the patterns of interaction that the child appears to bring naturally with him into the world.

The psychoanalytic approach 1 (Freud, 1960)

This focuses on instinctive behaviour of self-preservation, particularly the sex one. At each stage, sexual energy (*libido*) is invested in a specific part of the body (*erogenous zone*), and the maturational shift is triggered by changes in sensitivity of the different regions. The stages are as follows:

- 0–1 years: *oral (mouth)*
- 1–3 years: *anal (bottom)*
- 3–5 years: *phallic (genitals)*
- 5–12 years: *latency (resting period with own-sex relationships)*
- 12–18 years: *genital (sexual energy.)*.

In the *phallic* stage is the *Oedipal conflict*, in which the boy becomes aware of mother as a sex object and competes with father. The conflict is resolved when he *identifies* with father and represses feelings for mother. For girls, the conflict is different, as the original attachment is to mother with a shift to father. The broad outline of the development of attachments is accepted, but not the dynamics of the process.

The psychoanalytic approach 2 (Erikson, 1963)

This characterises changes in the child's motor and cognitive skills, and the impact these have on interactions. The stages have been described previously. The theory is influential, bringing together mental and personality development, and accounting for individual differences in interactions.

Social learning theories (Bandura et al., 1973)

These emphasise that the child's way of interacting with others is learned. Attachment is based on having needs met repeatedly with good things, so that the child sees the people who provide them as positive. Children do learn in ways that please adults and from observing models.

Cognitive-developmental theories (Kohlberg, 1966)

The behaviour of a child results from mental level. Changes in attachments are seen as the result of shifts in thinking ability.

Comment

Each theory offers strengths. The ethological one tells us about early interaction, while social learning concepts help us understand what happens over childhood. The cognitive-developmentalists point out the critical mental underpinnings to relations with others, while Erikson's psychoanalytic theory combines threads. Theories do not clarify the nature of a child's social interaction at home and school. Outside class, a child has many informal one-to-one and small-group exchanges in which responses are not judged as right or wrong. In these interactions, it is usually the child who controls, asking the questions for adults to answer, a situation which reverses in school. Children then talk only on an adult's direction. They are forced into a passive role and easily become anonymous. TAs, learning mentors and counsellors have opportunities to work with children in one-to-one situations or small groups. They can give pupils some control over the exchange and help to balance the large class situation, using approaches such as the Communication Opportunity Group Scheme (COGS) (Sage, 2000b).

Successful class interaction

Paulo Freire (1972) describes the ideal class interaction, which replaces the adult as the *sage on the stage with a guide by the side!*

Successful class interaction means all of the following:

1. Students express themselves, enabling them to hear each other's voices and opinions even if it is just saying their name.
2. External input is given by an adult expert on the topic.
3. Dialogue occurs in pairs, or small-group or large-group talk, depending on class size, to reflect and review the input.
4. Students, in pairs, summarise the topic content and record their summary, if possible, in words or drawings.

This model gives greater control in learning to the pupil. If valued and practised, it produces more able, interested and committed children, who view themselves as active participants. The way that the National Curriculum is presented results in emphasis on adult discourse in order to achieve curriculum objectives. We can really communicate effectively only if there is equality in interaction. This is the rule outside class, but not inside, and many pupils are frustrated by it.

Roles

Theories say little about *roles* affecting the exchange. A *role* is the part a person plays within a given situation. It requires certain behaviour, which defines the person's relationship with others in the group. For example, within the family, you may have the part of oldest daughter/son, sister/brother, niece/nephew and cousin. Custom gives you special responsibility, as your parents view you as a pillar of strength in family affairs, and so you expect to be taken into their confidence. As an older sibling, you feel responsible for younger ones. So each of these roles in the family entitles you to certain rights, but involves obligations too. Our positions determine whether we are a leader or follower in a group and give different opportunities to learn social skills.

We all play many roles in the course of our lives, as Jaques said in **As You Like It**: *All the world's a stage,/And all the men and women merely players;/They have their exists and their entrances; /And one man in his time plays many parts* (Act II, scene *vii*). Social scientists have attempted classifications. Basic roles depend on sex, age, position in the family and class, none of which is gained through merit. Occupational roles are largely achieved through our own efforts and may include the parts children play in school. If you are viewed as able, you are likely to be assigned leading roles, offering greater opportunities than for others who demonstrate fewer abilities.

TASK 2.6

HLTA 3.3.7 Recognise and respond effectively to equal opportunities issues as they arise, including by challenging stereotyped views, and by challenging bullying or harassment, following relevant policies and procedures.

Reflect on the different roles available for a child to play during the course of a day. You might produce an array like this for yourself:

family roles: daughter/son; sister/brother; cousin; granddaughter/-son; aunt/uncle

social roles: friend; acquaintance; team-mate; member of sports, drama, or music group, etc.

work role: educator; part-time student; other part-time worker.

Is the child's opportunity to play a variety of roles as wide as your own? What implications are there in your answer?

In social life, there is choice as to which role we adopt as we take account of the situation itself, the other person and ourselves. Situations prescribe roles clearly. Your friend is in hospital, and in the visitor role you bring comfort and support. The role will depend on a variety of factors and be influenced by things like age, gender, kinship, class and occupation. In school, you will have a role to play with colleagues, children and their parents. What are your expectations and how does your role influence how others respond to you? Pupils see teachers as authority figures, but since the role of a TA, learning mentor or counsellor is likely to be more intimate, they will view them as more like a parent, with a special, personal relationship. However, TAs have educative functions that expect children to respond to them correctly, and this may produce tension and stress in relationships (Diorio et al., 1993).

Finally, the role you choose depends on self-image, and at the beginning of any social encounter two people negotiate over those they adopt. Relationships are more harmonious if we make clear our role and accept those played by others. If a colleague is playing the earnest expert, and you persist in finding him funny, the interaction collapses. Choice of role has consequences. It affects how you dress, the way you speak and are spoken to, and the kinds of rights or obligations you expect, the sort of people you might encounter and so forth. If you regard yourself as an educated sophisticate, you will dress smartly and attractively, talk about serious ideas and expect to be invited to courses and lectures rather than football matches!

Understanding and diversifying our roles is an important part of development. Children in school play many parts, not only learner but also class star, fool or troublemaker. Some roles may deflect from their primary one as learner. Sage (2000a) looks at examples of children with learning problems and how their role as poor learners deprives them in subtle ways of opportunities to learn. Role-play is an important technique in learning. Children play adult roles of mothers and fathers/doctors and nurses to reach understanding of what it is like to be in these positions. To adopt an unfamiliar role demands empathy, so you might see an antagonist, such as a parent, teacher and policeman, in a new light and avoid conflicts. Try to make sure children experience working in many different groups that give them opportunities to play leader and follower roles. Also reverse roles in a task, so they are teaching you what they have learnt and can appreciate your part in the learning with greater understanding.

Review

The main ideas that define how processes and skills develop for communication and learning have been presented. There are different theories about this. All help us reflect more closely on a very complex process in which children bring together their physical, mental, emotional and social development as the base for achievements. There is a consensus that growth is a gradual process, based on innate potential and a positive environment. Many things interfere with this development, and some children arrive in schools without the foundation to learn. By considering theories, educators have knowledge to give appropriate input to children and encourage interesting and worthwhile responses that should not be judged as right or wrong, but as a valuable contribution to learning. Interventions are generally based on developmental guidelines, so using these frameworks can provide the right input for children.

Key Points

- Growth is gradual and thought to follow a developmental course.
- Communication depends on physical, mental, emotional and social components of learning.
- Aspects of learning integrate to support progression.
- Children achieve learning at different rates due to factors *within* and *without* the child that help or hinder progress.
- Learning requires positive communication and support from adults.
- Educators have a unique opportunity to develop effective communication and learning by giving children some control of the process and encouraging thinking and spoken communication.
- Key factors, including *personal and social qualities, decision making, communication, performance and numeracy/information technology*, are neglected in the curriculum drive for information.

How Can You Help Children to Communicate?

This chapter:

- considers the need to change our communication style if we are to encourage children to think and talk in the light of advice that four out of five comments from educators are negative (Wragg, 1994)
- explores how we can make a positive start to the above by questioning children in ways that do not require right or wrong answers
- recognises that children in school have varying abilities and backgrounds, and suggests that we need to present tasks that are suitable for a range of thinking and communicative levels
- shows that by understanding the nature of formal communication, which demands narrative thinking and structure, we can equip children to learn happily and successfully.

What do children need to help communication?

Life depends on our ability to communicate with other people. In class, therefore, our central concern should be how we communicate orally with children and how we facilitate this process of development. In reality, this is not so, as our main attention is given to reading and writing, although when children leave school, the focus will almost entirely be on speaking and listening. There are other probable reasons for our neglect of spoken communication. Can you think of some? Here are ideas that spring to mind:

- Communication is universal and ubiquitous (everywhere) and hard to capture and analyse.
- The results of communicating are not always apparent, as they affect the inner life of someone and appear intangible.

- Speech is here and gone, and is not as easily examinable as writing.
- Spoken communication is difficult to judge without extensive knowledge and training in a number of contributing medical, psychological and linguistic disciplines that enable precise evaluations of the manner, mode and movements that form verbal dynamics.

Thus, we are likely to believe that if spoken communication is neglected, no one will throw up their hands in horror! A few minutes in class proves the error of such an assumption, with pupils staring vacantly, behaving disruptively and performing poorly because of inappropriate and inadequate instruction. We think that since communication is natural, it will evolve effortlessly, but although a child has an in-built facility for this she needs opportunity to:

- Look, listen and reflect on good models of communication, in both informal and formal context.
- Imitate, try out and practise what is seen and heard.
- Clarify and control communication in interaction according to needs.
- Express feelings, ideas and views to develop thinking.
- Receive encouragement, coaching, sensitive correction and positive recognition for attempts.

If a child does not hear good models at home from parents who have intelligent, lively conversations and take an interest in the ability to understand and express, he will be either frustrated or inarticulate, unless the school assumes responsibility. Never has there been more need, as record numbers of children are arriving in school with inadequate communication, and research suggests that 75% of them are possibly at risk (Sage, 2000a).

There is an old saying that when a whole family is responsible for feeding the dog, it often goes hungry, and this is similar to the situation in schools. In a maths lesson, for example, the teacher may be too preoccupied with accuracy to worry about the way facts are presented, or how they are represented and related in a child's mind. Therefore, in addition to incidental work that might be possible, communication must be treated as a subject in its own right that is directly concerned with the pupil's interests and personality. The COGS, discussed in Chapter 1, follows this philosophy and some countries, such as Japan, have proved its importance by giving communication status, resulting in high levels of attainment.

If we do consider communication in school, generally it is superficially in relation to speech sounds, vocabulary or grammar performance, or in relation to speaking and listening components. There is nothing wrong with this, but it leaves areas of communicative experience untouched. In spite of advances in knowledge regarding teaching the 'whole child', we still devote most attention to the parts of a pupil that analyse and compute. The bits that feel, imagine, create and enjoy are given less importance, leading to split personalities. Therefore, we miss out on the integrating and unifying features of talk that employ body, brain, mind and spirit. The more opportunities and value we give to communication in classrooms, the more we are counteracting the disruptive tendencies in education, which treat facts separately from feelings and dish out bits of information in boxes. Under the National Curriculum, we are forced to think of subjects rather than children. Their needs and characteristics are off-timetable in today's world, but if we are to raise achievement, we must acknowledge the need for:

- adventure, fun and self-expression
- positive relationships that can inform, motivate, encourage and support
- positive and constructive feedback on performance
- communicating thoughts, feelings and views
- constant physical activity
- development of interaction, participation and social sense
- imagination and creation
- intellectual curiosity stimulated from rich experiences
- enjoyment of movement, rhythm, and repetition
- collection, making things and learning from active experience.

Education in communication (as in the COGS) satisfies these needs and helps expression through talk and oral games; physical activity through role-play; social sense through discussion; imagination through creative opportunities; intellectual curiosity through question-and-answer activities; movement and rhythm through choral speaking opportunities; and desire for adventure and active experience through news, storytelling and reporting. Communicating is thus the main factor in teaching the art of living, loving, belonging, knowing, believing and doing.

Classroom situations

What is the most essential thing for successful classroom learning? Surely, it is attitude of mind. Whatever aspect of education we take and whatever stage, the rapport between educators and learners is all-important. Communication is how we establish this relationship, and what is said and done, and how, are a reflection of the speaker's mind, feelings and imagination – the whole of his person in fact. We develop and demonstrate our personalities through talk. The adult most likely to succeed in helping children learn is the one who is interested in the lives, thoughts, feelings, responses and contributions of pupils. Such adults respect each child as an individual, showing positive value for the different personalities and talents in a group. They create an atmosphere that is comforting and comfortable, in which fluent speech can naturally grow.

Atmosphere defies definition, but one is immediately aware of its presence or absence. With it comes a sense of kindness, courtesy and friendly cooperation between adults and children, that is positive, promoting well-being and self-esteem. Classroom situations, however, are unreal for children, and if we want to produce effective responses from them, we need to resemble as far as possible the actual world we inhabit. We are likely to talk easily if we:

- do not feel constraint about using our voices to express
- converse with others on equal terms with chance to control the interaction
- engage, involve and share something that interests us
- want to hear what others have to say
- are not expected to talk for too long
- are not interrupted or put down by others
- are confident and competent about speaking in public
- are practised in the rules and moves of informal and formal communication.

However sympathetic adults try to be, they will remain something of an 'oracle' to pupils, who will generally be reticent about challenging the one who knows! It is important, therefore, to make every opportunity for children to talk among themselves and share their knowledge. The smaller the working group – down to a pair – the greater the relevance of the talk. The more experienced the class is in this way of working, the more useful consultation there is between groups and with adults in class.

The ignorance of a newcomer is the greatest stimulus for talk, so making chances for parents, friends and others to come and listen to presentations on trips or projects works wonders for developing narrative thinking and structure. This is common school practice in Japan, where they value communication above the curriculum. We do not normally tell something to someone who already knows, and too often children are asked to present familiar information, which results in a halting performance because of boredom. Let's consider how to help children become confident communicators.

Helping communication in class

In classrooms, educators see their major role as delivering new information to children, so that checking whether this has been assimilated is judged important. The following section makes suggestions to make the process more successful.

Questions and answers

It is surprising how seldom we analyse questioning activity, as it takes up a large amount of class time. How we frame questions is important for effective answers.

TASK 3.1A

HLTA 3.2.3 Monitor pupils' participation and progress, providing feedback to teachers, and giving constructive support to pupils as they learn.

Try asking children a questions such as *What animal barks?*

Then frame the question in a more open way: *What do we know about dogs?*

Record the range of answers, such as: *They are pets; There are lots of different types; We have a dog, Basil, at home; My favourite dog is a Jack Russell.*

(Continued)

(Continued)

If we say, *What animal barks?* we shall get only the word 'dog' in reply. However, if we ask in a more open way, *What do we know about dogs?*, we are likely to achieve a range of answers. This type of question, therefore, facilitates a range of ideas, and encourages thinking. However, children must be able to *explain* in order to answer an *open* question. The use of a *closed* question demanding a one-word answer (*What is your favourite dog?*) focuses on a specific aspect of a situation and is appropriate for pupils who have limited communication. Such questions are judged right or wrong, and make children nervous about answering incorrectly.

It is important to regard questions as a whole-class situation, and not a one-to-one experience with the adult in charge. For this reason, we must encourage pupils to answer so that everyone can hear. Children will quickly get into the habit of speaking louder, slower and clearer if this is insisted upon. It helps them to achieve if an example is modelled and the response is coached as shown below.

TA: *Jo, I've shown you how to say: **The moon is round**, by moving the vowel and sounds in the words 'moon' and 'round', by slowing the 'oo' and the 'ou' down and building up sound. You have a try – creating a picture of what the words mean by the way you say them.*

Jo: *The moon is round.*

TA: *You really made the moon feel round with how you moved the 'oo' and 'ou' sounds. Try again to make your voice louder so that Mark in the back corner can hear you easily. Show that you really like telling us this fact!*

TASK 3.1B

Follow up the work above by modelling and encouraging effective communication of ideas to peers in a similar way to the above example.

What is the purpose of questions?

Reflecting on the purpose of questions is necessary because the ping-pong nature of the factual ones is more a test of memory than learning. If the aim is to check how much has been understood, it is more effective to achieve this indirectly through discussion, which allows judgement of how much information has been absorbed. And why not change places with pupils sometimes?

TASK 3.2

HLTA 3.2.2 They monitor pupils' responses to learning tasks and modify their approach accordingly.

Change places with the pupils. Get them to question you. Analyse the kind of questions they ask.

Children feel driven to remember facts, but if interested in a topic, they may be keen to know more. Questions asked by pupils will indicate how far we have succeeded in creating interest and enquiry, and will stimulate them to clarify thinking. Answering pupils' questions is an effective method of supplying just the right amount of information they need at a given time. Adults satisfy the curiosity of children and their desire to know and understand more about the world in which they live. The idea that school is a place where only educators question is contrary to the reality outside class where commonly children ask and adults provide answers. Obviously, this makes sense, as it is educators who should know the answers and children who need to question to gain information.

Children should also ask more questions of each other. In a talk where the speaker is hesitant, a question from another will prevent drying up and keep words flowing. When a group leader reports to the whole class what has been discussed, there must be chance for others to query. In true discussion, the children talk more than the adults, and their speech is directed to peers.

However, real discussion, where speakers are able to put forward a point of view with others confirming or contradicting it with evidence, is a sophisticated, advanced narrative thinking level. In a class/group situation, educators need constantly to produce experiences that tap into the whole range of thinking levels, because varying pupil ages and stages will mean they operate at different points on the cognitive and linguistic continuum. The following section presents some examples of what can be done to facilitate the range of narrative thinking stages.

Level 1: record: producing ideas

Unless we easily produce a range of ideas about something, it is difficult to develop any sense of their arrangement or make a judgement about them. Therefore, continually encouraging the expression of attributes kick-starts thinking. Ability to describe is essential to talking formally, as in giving a set of instructions, an explanation or telling or retelling of experiences. It is also the process that takes you into writing, as the following comparison of speech and written text indicates.

> **Informal speaking**: Context – Rosie and Helen are doing a last-minute wander before their garden is open under the National Gardens Scheme.

> **Rosie (speaking to Helen)**: *They're the size of dinner plates!*

> **Formal writing**: Rosie and Helen are in the garden looking at some giant sunflowers, which they have grown from seed. Both are amazed at the size of the blooms, and Rosie remarks, *They're the size of dinner plates!*

The written account makes up for the fact that anyone reading it cannot see events, so the place, people and actions have to be described and pictured to be understood. However, much information is missing, such as the age, size, physical appearance, relationship, personality, and mood of Rosie and Helen; the house and garden layout; the locality (urban or rural); the weather; the time of day and year; and the wider context – are there others present? – is it a casual occasion or is the garden open for charity/etc. If the context is not present, as in formal speech or writing, the audience has to make up for information and opinion gaps by using inference that allows them to bring both the context and events together to make sense. Imagination and experience are required in huge measure because meaning lies behind, rather than in, words themselves.

This process of informal to formal communication operates as a continuous activity of both cognitive and linguistic development known as narrative thinking and structure. This needs to be understood and addressed specifically and developmentally in teaching routines for children to move effortlessly from speaking to writing. Some ideas for helping this process are listed here.

- If you are introducing a learning topic (such as **Healthy food**), have actual examples present and ask pupils to select one from those supplied. Pass the object around so all can see and feel, and ask everyone to say one thing about it. If working with a small group, you can go round repeatedly for as long as pupils can bring up ideas. It is useful to nominate one child to keep a tally of ideas expressed (the most I have totalled is 309 in response to a hologram disc I bought at Universal Studios, Hollywood!). When the responses started to resemble ideas already expressed – I would liven up the process with a comment: *I think the hologram would make me a lovely earring*, starting off a completely new train of thought with the group! The number of ideas can be recorded and compared in a graph with similar activities. Communication switches constantly between speaking, listening, reading and writing, and all modes should be considered together if possible. As literacy and numeracy are secondary language activities, expressing information in graphics and numerics instead of phonemes (word sounds), they need to be introduced in contexts that are meaningful, so that children can understand their application. This is important because Ewers-Rogers (1992) has shown that children have problems in applying numbers in real situations because they have not been introduced in meaningful ways.

- If you are introducing or reinforcing a topic, prime children before and encourage them to bring into school anything they might have to illustrate this. Ask for small objects that can go in a box. If working with a whole class, divide it into groups of about 6-8 and have a box for each group in which to place the objects they have brought. Play music (a pupil can be put in charge) and pass the box around the circle. When the music stops, the child with the box has to take out an object (not their own) and say what they can about it in 30 seconds (another child can be in charge of timing). The adult's role is to observe child responses and identify those who have difficulty expressing a range of attributes. This is the fundamental level of narrative thinking, and no child can progress without this intact. This game is popular with all ages.

- Make creative thinking a regular class/group/individual challenge. Take something that cannot be obviously named, such as a *black blob,* and ask participants to come up with ideas of what they think it is. Keep the score on the door, and at the term's end the group/child with the most points for these challenges is awarded a prize (a yard of chocolate, with eight bars is popular and can be equally shared). This imaginative ability has to be fostered and the pay-offs are pupils who can produce ideas effortlessly to take into writing.

Level 2: recite: arrange ideas in a limited way, but not in time sequence

When children can produce a range of ideas about something, they naturally start to structure them in some way. Using the previous topic, (**Healthy foods**), produce a shopping basket with the following items:

apple, cheese, salmon (tin), porridge, carrot, honey, lemon, sardines (tin), baked beans (tin), eggs, butter, banana, potato, tuna (tin), orange, onion, milk, bread and nuts.

The activity can be done as an individual, group or class exercise. Children should be encouraged to discover their own categories in which to slot objects. If this is done as an individual exercise, follow up with a paired one so children can discuss and compare choices more widely. Then one pair can be put with another to extend comparisons.

Possible groups may be *fruit, vegetables, fish, sweet things, things coming from cows, breakfast foods, snack foods,* and *things liked or disliked.*

Categorising the goods will produce discussion and possible dissension, but if this is done as a group exercise, it encourages negotiation and decision. In the review, pupils should share reflections and, if there is time, choose their favourite food, and mime it for others to guess. This reinforces non-verbal communication and helps to develop powers of inference for understanding formal talk or text.

In most teaching, categorising plays a part, so devising activities that highlight this continually and continuously sharpens judgement. Giving children a chance to express choices develops meta-cognition. It is a difficult concept, but it means ability to reflect on behaviour and awareness of what is involved in doing something. This high-level ability is necessary for advanced learning and monitoring one's own performance.

Level 3: refer: compare ideas

Once children can sort ideas according to criteria, they can proceed to making comparisons of similarity and difference in a more advanced way. Here are some suggestions.

- Put children in pairs, back to back, and have each paired child in turn report on what the other is wearing, so that they have to recall through visualisation. Then get them to discuss similarities and differences between the clothing sets because, even though they might be in uniform, there will be differences in size, colour, style or material to identify.

- Ask children to discuss things that make them happy or sad, and compare group choices to discover similarities and differences. These can be expressed graphically and numerically, since part of interactive communication is teamwork – planning and producing results that can be expressed in spoken or written forms. Every opportunity should be taken to reinforce these broader notions of communication, known as key skills, although *skill* is a misnomer, as cognitive *process* is the accurate representation of what is involved. *Process* is a connected, continuous natural action, whereas *skill* is doing something well. Therefore, *process* defines the phenomenon and *skill* the way it is performed. For example, reading is a process in which we are skilled, semi-skilled or unskilled. If we reduce process to skill in our minds, we fail to understand the nature of the set of continuous events, by just focusing on performance. The shift is from informal to formal speaking and then into writing. Since this oracy-to-literacy move is not viewed as continuous, children are thrust into written activities before they have acquired informal and formal speaking. This happens regularly in today's education system. Children are asked to perform written tasks that are beyond thinking and speaking levels (case studies in Sage, 2000a).
- If you establish a review period after an activity, you have an opportunity to compare facts and opinions, with pupils encouraged to sum up what has been expressed in terms of these criteria. Facts and opinions form the basis of evaluation, and it is difficult to encourage children to do this at higher levels, suggesting that the narrative process has not been specifically taught and regularly practised for conscious and confident reflection.

Level 4: replay: sequence ideas in time

This level is often a sticking point for children who have learning problems because they find it difficult to move thinking from present to past and future time. Luria and Yudovich (1968) have called this problem *synpraxia,* and it is common in primary pupils. It will be witnessed in child language if the past or future tense is not signalled and events are expressed in present tense only. Here is an example of a 6-year-old boy, Mark, talking about his trip to his grandparents on the previous day:

> *I go Gramp's and Gran's house.(3) I see Rory and Ralph (cousins).(2) We go to park.(5) I watch football match and eat dinner.(4) I dig holes and plant seeds. They're sunflowers.(1)*

The authenticity of events was checked with Mark's mum. The seed planting happened first, followed by seeing the cousins, who dropped by on their way shopping. The visit to the grandparents happened at 2.30 pm, and as Liverpool (Gramp's favourite team) was playing, they had lunch watching the match followed by a play on the swings in the park nearby.

Mark has chosen from a range of events that had happened the day before, but he has not presented these in the correct time frame. His language gives a clue to his lack of awareness of time space, as all five events are expressed in present tense. When Mark's performance was investigated further, it appeared that he was not adept at sorting or comparing things, so this was reinforced in level 2 and 3 activities within a weekly COGS group in school. It is logical that children must have a well-developed ability to compare attributes if they are to move from area to time space easily. Once this narrative level was established for Mark, it was much easier to work on the concept of time within the framework of a day – selecting one thing at breakfast, one at lunch and one at bedtime as reference points. The expression of these events in the past tense was established before considering the same exercise in a future event such as tomorrow. The relation of cognitive and linguistic competence is clearly illustrated, and the importance of considering these together is fully established.

This activity may be varied according to requirements. Children can be asked in class/group one thing they did well yesterday, one today and one they hope to do tomorrow, so the concept of events outside present time can be reinforced.

Level 5: recount: explain ideas – how? why?

This level flows naturally from the last, but comprehending the order of events and how they fit to achieve a goal takes the thinking a step further. Explaining how to make a sandwich, or a cup of tea, or to clean a pair of shoes, depends on understanding how and why events occur. You cannot make tea if the articles needed have not been gathered and tasks ordered correctly. For example, the kettle must be filled with cold water before it is boiled. A child will have grasped cause and effect to achieve a correct sequence at this level. At stage 4, the preservation of exact order is not necessary to retell the events of a day, a trip, an experience, etc. These steps in narrative thinking are important not only to consider but also to fully comprehend and implement within classroom practice.

The fact that some school leavers have not achieved this narrative level is reported in the literature and by the Confederation of British Industry website. Inability to give instructions is a familiar complaint about employees and evidence that these higher-thinking levels have not been grasped.

Give pupils the opportunity to explain how to do things. Instead of doing this yourself, as the adult in charge, allow them to give familiar instructions about lining up for assembly or catching a bus for swimming lessons. They do this in Japan, and if you give pupils control they not only behave well, but also rise to the occasion.

TASK 3.3

HLTA 3.3.1 Using clearly structured teaching and learning activities, they interest and motivate pupils, and advance their learning.

Design an opportunity to enable pupils to give others instructions in a meaningful context. Make time to discuss afterwards how improvements can be made.

Level 6 : report: discuss ideas – giving an opinion

In giving a report, the importance of descriptive language comes into its own, as visualising to retain and recall information is reinforced. When an event has been described so that it can be seen in the mind's eye, you then can give opinion and reflection. This depends upon being objective about the situation and demonstrating different points of view before drawing conclusions based on attitudes, values and experience. Start off by encouraging visualisation to conjure up detail. Bell (1991) and Sage (2003) both stress the importance of picturing something to make the information meaningful in order to remember it. Both researchers suggest that children who fail to learn have limited visualisation abilities.

- Ask pupils to close their eyes for a minute and imagine a white screen on their foreheads. Instruct them to concentrate hard and see what pops onto the screen, raising their hands when they have a picture. Pupils can swap descriptions in pairs. In the whole-class group, suggest that two or three pupils share their pictures. This focuses on the descriptive process, which can be recorded in a picture, words, or whatever way pupils choose.
- Mock television reports are often a popular way to improve reporting abilities if there is a video camera at hand. Pupils can be put in groups with roles of camera operator, producer, producer's assistant, presenter, etc., and asked to organise a report lasting two minutes on something that interests them or a topic of study. They must provide a brief description, giving a comment that reflects a range of views before establishing their own opinion. Using video gives feedback, so that pupils can see themselves in action and assess the pros and cons of their performances.
- Although debates may be better left to secondary schools, when children have established an ability to be objective and decisive, there is advantage in posing questions on issues such as *Keeping animals as pets* in order to help children understand different points of view and establish their own position within the range of arguments. Children often try to score points rather than seek the truth, and this must be discussed so that everyone can understand the benefits of listening respectfully and seriously to what others say.

Level 7: relate: tell a story with setting, events, actions, reactions, conclusions and reflections

This level puts together all the narrative components honed to perfection on previous ones! Retelling stories is regarded by many as a ghastly ritual, but it is a reliable guide to a child's cognitive and linguistic competence and should be treated imaginatively. Ask for the class to vote for a favourite story and then in groups of six be responsible for a specific episode to present. For example, if the story is *Cinderella*, tell it to the children first to establish the storyline and then structure the parts that make up the whole narrative:

1. **The setting**: Cinderella's home and her ugly sisters
2. **Events**: the invitation to the prince's ball and preparations to attend
3. **Actions**: the fairy godmother, dress and coach; the ball, and the prince dancing with Cinderella
4. **Reactions**: midnight and Cinderella's flight; the prince's search
5. **Conclusion**: the prince finds Cinderella
6. **Reflections**: bad situations can get better!

Children have fun putting together a performance and should be encouraged to use the above or a similar format. This helps them understand the unity of events and how they fit together and take apart. Very shy children or those with a communication problem can be paired and assigned a non-speaking role. Once pupils have decided on the content for their section, they can produce props to enliven the performance.

This teaches children the way in which a continuous narrative is composed and ensures that all are aware of what is expected of them. The actual telling, however, should be in the children's own words and in the way they want to express these.

Another approach is to vary the length of a story already presented to children by contracting or expanding the narrative. So, the group could take *Cinderella* and work out how to tell the 10-minute story in three minutes. Here is an example of a traditional tale that children have enjoyed expanding:

> *Zut was a boy who lived in Zulu with his father and mother, the king and queen. They were happy except for one thing: Zut would pull faces. Everyone told him that his face would get stuck and it did. Wizards, witches, doctors and dentists tried to straighten Zut's face but all failed. One clever man said the only cure was to see a face as ugly as his own. The king offered a reward and everyone hurried to the palace to make an ugly face, but no one was quite as ugly as Zut. Then one day, he was walking sadly in the garden and looked into a pool. There, Zut saw a face as ugly as his. He was cured instantly and never pulled an ugly face again.*

Pupils are given a few minutes to think how they would tell the story, and then four are sent out of class. They return one by one and tell their own version supplying what details they choose. The attention is kept because the stories are all so different, and the class can discuss this in the review part of the lesson.

Another variation is to tell an old, familiar story. Most children in the Midlands have heard of Robin Hood and his merry band who robbed the rich to give to the poor. In our rich, celebrity culture with an opposing underclass, the story has a modern ring.

Select children to be Robin Hood, Maid Marion, Friar Tuck and Little John, who are the main characters in the narrative. Robin tells Friar Tuck to call his followers (the class group) to a clearing in the forest (the centre of the room). Robin addresses them, saying they are going to hear about events that have happened to the outlaw band. He asks for a volunteer as the first storyteller. The children then can come forward in turn and create or re-create the many tales told about Robin Hood and his merry band, and all can be actively involved in the telling. The more that they can enter into the spirit of the scenes and act the part of creative listeners, the more successful the storytelling.

Developing narrative thinking through discussion

It is important to be aware that there are many narrative levels – in our model, seven have been identified. Understanding that narrative thinking and structure are continuous processes helps us to select activities for children that are appropriate to their own stage of development. Normally children fail because they are given tasks that are beyond their cognitive and linguistic capacity. In the next section, we reflect in more detail about discussion, because this is the teaching style to implement for facilitating thinking, communicating and learning, but it needs careful handling to be successful.

A good discussion depends on conversation, which is a neglected art. In schools, educators talk to children, who might occasionally reply, but this cannot accurately be described as proper discourse, as adults dominate and control the action. As Pooh Bear complained, *That isn't conversing – not first one and then the other!* but this kind of talking is common in many contexts. Good conversation is a situation where there is equal control between participants, and the topic is taken up, commented on and extended, so that all benefit from a true exploration of ideas and different viewpoints are expressed.

Discussion

Discussion is the most important communication activity for learning, as it:

- creates a lively interest by airing a range of contrasting views
- enlarges knowledge by sharing and reflecting on information
- helps children to know others and their interests and to consider the environment
- teaches respect and consideration for the views of others
- trains the clear thinking and coherent expression needed for the development of narrative thinking and structure.

Discussion also provides training for the *middle* language that is halfway between playground slang and bookish English – the type of formal language needed for learning. The best discussions arise spontaneously from current events – just after a trip out, on hearing local news, or at the announcement of something exciting such as the circus coming to town! The children's natural excitement fires up their minds. However, one can arouse a similar feeling by subjects such as history or geography, as dialogue can be used to collect information and provide insight into pupils' personalities and opinions while checking on what has been assimilated.

Discussion takes two forms: whole-class discussion under adult direction, and the group type when small sets of pupils work simultaneously on the same thing or on different topics in either different or mixed ability forums. It is useful in small-group discussions to arrange a whole-class plenary and elect a leader to present a summary of the consensus. This allows an enormous amount of information to be shared and reviewed.

Whole-class discussion

This is a good starting point, as it enables an adult to model good practice and set the pattern for small-group activities. They can create an atmosphere, that will produce lively but serious talk. The over-talkative child can be restrained, and the shy, hesitant one encouraged. In order to make discussion work, it is essential to:

1. be clear about what is being discussed
2. limit the ground to be covered.

For example, if we ask children what they think about the video they have just seen on the tsunami disaster, they are likely to answer: *Bad, Upsetting, Scary*. These do not reinforce an impression or increase a pupil's ability to express views. As an alternative, suppose we take one aspect at a time:

- **setting**: Asia; coastal regions; climate; types of dwellings
- **story**: eruption of giant plates; massive wave; devastation; rescue activities
- **people**: adults; children; tourists; things that happened to them; how they coped; the problems experienced; the population's work, dress, future, etc.
- **our reactions**: feelings, views, knowledge of the area; handling disasters; what we can learn from the experience; comparisons with other world events.

This allows children to focus minds, relive the experience, and bring into play their feelings and imagination. When they speak, they will have many things to talk about, which will be ordered and relayed with animation. This does mean some preparation by the adult in charge, who must decide the headings for discussion – although it might be possible to draw these out from the class and get them to set the agenda. At the very least, the adult needs to create the scene and provide a few signposts that set pupils on their way. Getting the class, for example, to recall and describe something awful that has happened, in order to draw out general points about coping helps orientate minds to disasters. We have all had some experience of them. The children could be put in groups briefly to think up questions that they want answered, such as *What would you do if your house was smashed to bits?* or *What do you need to survive when you have lost everything?* Having decided the field for discussion, the whole class, will then consider points one by one. The adult's role is to provide a summary of what has been said. After practice in the class group, children should be ready to tackle discussion in smaller forums.

Group discussion of a topic

This has strong advantages as more ground can be covered in the same time and individuals have more chance to talk. This is the perfect format to develop leadership and examine roles and relationships in the group. Nominating one or two children to observe group behaviour is essential in order to draw attention to aspects of effective working. Notice who did the most talking, who was missed out of the dialogue, how problems were resolved; how ideas progressed, etc.

The procedure is as follows. Begin with whole-class talk after you have introduced the topic. Have the class briefly comment, and select headings for detailed discussion with support. For example: *Our class is having a day for parents and friends to see what we do.* Headings may emerge as follows:

1. When is it best to have the day?
2. What sort of events should we offer?
3. How would we display our class activities?
4. Do we need refreshments? If so what, when and how would we prepare them?
5. If children come, how could we keep them happy and entertained?
6. What are the jobs to be done and how do we decide roles?

Six headings would generate topics for six groups of 5–6 pupils, with one elected as leader. They should be asked to set rules for discussion, and the leader' role must be clarified. Make sure all have a chance to speak, keep order, review what has been said, and summarise final results and reactions.

Contrary to expectation, discipline problems seldom arise if pupils are responsible for their own actions. The more engaged they are, the less noise they will make, although animated talk creates a working buzz!

The adult/s should move from group to group, checking that the leader is encouraging everyone to take part and answering questions that arise. At first, a natural leader will emerge in the group, but, gradually all children should be helped to accept this role. The discussion lasts for around five minutes, allowing a great deal of talk. Then the leaders report on their group's findings, standing up so that their voice carries to the whole class. The leaders need to be reminded that they are addressing other groups, and not the teacher, who may need to move behind the furthest-away child to discourage this tendency.

After the leader has spoken, other members should add comments, with the class free to question and comment. Finally, the adult summarises and adds appropriate reflections.

In Japan, group discussions are part of all lessons, and the final review sees *every* child making a comment on what they feel about the experience. Although, this is less of a tradition in England, it should be encouraged if we really want to deepen thinking and expression and raise pupil standards.

Discussion begins to work after about 3–4 trials and must become a regular feature of classroom practice if one is to reap results in improved pupil performance.

> **TASK 3.4**
>
> *HLTA 3.3.5 Advance pupils' learning in a range of classroom settings, including working with individuals, small groups and whole classes where the assigned teacher is not present.*
>
> Initiate a discussion using one of the models above. Show how you have planned, before hand, some specific aspects related to the topic to help children focus. If possible, compare the outcomes, the quality of talk, and the level of motivation and enthusiasm with a discussion that was not so structured.

Group discussion on different topic dimensions

Once the class is familiar with discussion as a way to learn, the format can be varied. After setting the scene with a brief introduction, the six headings are decided, but instead of discussing the *whole* subject, each group discusses *one* of the six aspects. It works best if children join the group that is talking about the dimension of greatest interest to them. This approach saves time and makes it possible to tackle aspects in depth, leading to less overlapping in reporting back.

It is useful to suggest the continuation of the discussion at home and ask pupils to bring back parents' views for a later lesson. This helps to create a bond between home and school and establish this type of talk outside the four walls of the classroom. *Should everyone help with home chores?* is a good topic.

Discussing with support staff

Often support staff take groups for specific purposes, such as extra reinforcement for a lesson recently taught, but the rules for discussion can still be used to conduct effective talk. Some children will not have achieved conversational skills and need to be placed in pair situations in order to develop listening and responding. Maybe they will be unable to discuss without props to prompt ideas. So, if they are asked to talk about making a list of things needed for survival – a picture of a devastating scene will aid thinking and a number of objects such as a bottle of water, a blanket, plasters, etc., will give them things to touch that can activate memories.

Discovery groups

This variation begins with six speakers who give a 2-minute talk on something that interests them. The adult checks that topics are not the same to ensure a varied programme. After the talks, six groups are formed, with the speaker hot-seating – answering questions from the rest. It is obviously sensible for children to join the group that most appeals. The session ends with another group member providing a review of the gathered information for the whole class. As children should be assessed for oral as well as written performance, the class can draw up two aspects of a good presentation (*clear facts; performance that keeps everyone listening*) and an effective working group (*all said something; task completed*). Pupils are encouraged to rank performances from

5 = excellent through to 1= could do better. The small groups mark for effective working while the whole class assesses the presentations. Marks are totalled by pupils, and means are recorded. When children assess themselves, they learn to understand expected standards and gain a better appreciation of how to achieve them.

TASK 3.5

HLTA 3.3.3 Promote and support the inclusion of all pupils in the learning activities in which they are involved.

Design an opportunity for pupils to engage in assessing each other.

Project groups

These work well for children who are over 7 years old, as the work extends over several periods, requiring the ability to keep ideas in mind over time. A theme arises out of a visit, discussion or lesson, and after class review, all children conduct their own research on an aspect that interests them. After two sessions, the teacher assesses progress in a lesson where everyone has a minute to speak about the collected information. This gives an opportunity to group those with similar interests with a brief for a public presentation after another 6–8 lessons.

This approach is common in Japan, where pupils are given great freedom to work where and how they like (library, outside, other free space, etc.), resulting in their communicating ideas, planning and working together, and producing a team effort, and this fosters community and pride. It provides a natural format for the contextual use of both spoken and written components of communication, and because work is under the children's control, there is more motivation and enthusiasm to succeed. Class unity, accompanied by the right attitudes and techniques for discussion, is an essential aspect of the success of this method. Children today often come to school with no conversational abilities – no notion of turn taking, listening to others, or following a topic thread – so that discussions may take time to become established and be effective. They are worth pursuing through the pain barrier, however, as they are the key to engaged and enhanced performances by pupils.

Teaching communication to children

In subject lessons, coaching in communication is largely incidental. We can, however, achieve results as long as we believe the child is more important than the subject, and every chance is given for pupil-talk in pairs, in groups and to the whole class. There are also many opportunities available in the social life of school, where children can show visitors around, take messages, return registers to the office, announce on the public address system, organise fund raising, arrange book clubs, talk at assemblies, etc. This incidental work, however, is not sufficient. The problem with subject teaching is that educators are listening for evidence of correct information, and pupils are asked to talk about something they have only just heard about and not fully assimilated. In social activity, the emphasis is on action, and not the quality of the talk, so neither of these two experiences is enough to develop the communication process that is needed to sustain high personal and academic standards.

It is therefore important to have a time each week when topics of general or strong personal interest can be concentrated on for effective expression and communication, and the format of the COGS is strongly recommended for this, as it is based on the development of ideas (narrative thinking) and how they are expressed (narrative structure), so that children have the best chance to match cognitive and linguistic progress. Unless pupils have the opportunity for specific teaching and coaching in communication that can lay stronger foundations for secondary language developments, we will continue to wrestle with the problem of raising standards. The next chapter looks at developing specific speaking techniques that help effectiveness.

Key Points

- Spoken communication is the way we conduct life's business, but it takes second place to literacy in educational practice.
- Children need time to talk in order to develop thinking and expression.
- When working with children, we need to be aware of their different thinking and communication stages.
- A model of narrative thinking and structure successfully differentiates tasks for children and allows them to work at a level at which they can achieve success as well as having the opportunity to observe activities at further points along the continuum.
- Equal opportunity for children and adults to express ideas and opinions is the classroom style that achieves success, but this needs a guided approach, as many children have limited conversational skills.
- TAs can develop their role of helping children access learning by becoming aware of the communicative process and how to facilitate this both informally and formally.

What Techniques Develop Speaking?

This chapter:

- shows that to focus on children's speech may seem old-fashioned, but that the pay-off in enhanced comprehension is substantial
- examines voice control and variation techniques that make words come alive
- suggests exercises that can be practised at regular intervals for 5–10 minutes, resulting in, for instance, a chance for the group or class to bond together in choral speaking.

Attitudes to speaking well

Speaking involves more muscles than any other human activity, and yet we probably dismiss people who exercise these as rather odd. But as a colleague once remarked, *Why should P.E. stop at the neck?* Children need technical practice to gain control and flexibility in speech as well as in sports, music, art and design, which also depend on physical agility. So far, we have concentrated on thinking, feeling and imagination, and their verbal and non-verbal expression. At the same time, technique is important because it acts as the bridge between speaker and listener. Now we can justify the use of the term *skill* as a measure of our speaking performance! Communication has no value unless it can make the impression we intend and touch the minds and hearts of those who are listening. If others cannot hear us because we are unable to project our voices, cannot distinguish our words because of our careless pronunciation, misunderstand us through the wrong emphasis we give to words, or are bored because our voices are tuneless, monotonous and dull, then we have failed as speakers, however good the matter is we are attempting to convey.

Technical exercises help physical control required for clear, fluent and interesting talk.

Development of speech expression

The best halfway house between mechanical exercise and interpretation is the speech rhyme. Lip, tongue and breathing exercises are boring for youngsters, but verses that are fun bring the advantage of established content so that performance can be targeted. Rhymes need careful selection to show a natural use of language and a striking turn of phrase and can be chosen to reflect the content of a particular lesson or an ongoing theme. The story below was used successfully to strengthen the *tongue tip*, through the practice of the voiceless plosive sound – *t*. This is underdeveloped in many children because their attention has not been drawn to the manner, place and articulation of speech. Practice helps precise movements that also assist the development of other sounds that use the tongue tip, such as *d, th, s, z*.

TA: Hello, everyone. My neighbour, Sue, has a pony called Jock, and every day she takes him for a walk before school. First, he ambles along and his hard hooves tap on the road.

Class: *Click with front of tongue firmly and strongly on the ridge behind front teeth*: t–t, t–t, t–t-...

TA: Soon, Sue turns off the road into a lane and Jock, starts to trot.

Class: *Click firmly and quickly*: t–t, t–t, t–t...

TA: At the bottom of the lane is a gate into a field. It is open, and Jock is excited at the stretch of green field in front of him. He starts to gallop.

Class: *Quicker but with less volume but keeping sounds clear*: tttt – tttt – tttt ...

TA: Sue draws on the reins and Jock comes to a halt. It's time to go home and get ready for school. Back up the lane they both go.

Class: *Slow plodding*: t – t – t...

TA: Can we make up a rhyme to remember Jock's walk?

> *Clipperty, clop, clipperty clop,*
>
> *Sue's brown pony is ready to flop.*
>
> *He's been out for a walk,*
>
> *No... not for a talk,*
>
> *His feet on the track,*
>
> *Clickity-clack, clickity-clack.*

Although contrived, a few minutes of sound play will help focus on the consonant sounds that shape words and how they can be performed to create strong images. After examples, the group will soon suggest a story or incident of their own to build around sound practice. Ten, 20 or 30 heads are better than one, and ideas soon start flowing.

> **TASK 4.1**
>
> *HLTA 1.2 Build and maintain successful relationships with pupils, treat them consistently, with respect and consideration, and be concerned for their development as learners.*
>
> Encourage children in a group or class to share alternatives and build a story around their ideas, as above.

Suggestions to focus on voice production and variation as a follow-up to the sound story are explored below (see Table 4.1). It is a good idea to begin a session by practising relaxation and control parts of the body in the following 30-second routine.

Relaxation

Stand with legs about 20 cm apart and hands loosely by the side. Have weight just a little over the balls of the feet so that the body is in the line of gravity and is in a relaxed posture. Imagine you are a piece of elastic about to be stretched. Talk the group through this differential tension and releasing: *Stretch from your toes, through feet to heels, up through lower legs to knees, through upper legs to thighs; stretch your waist at least 10 cm and through to your chest, stretch up through your arms, to your wrists and fingers. Imagine a string gently pulling your head and arms upward. There's a man with a big scissors ready to cut the strings and let you flop gently down from the waist. Now you are like a rag doll – loose and floppy! Draw yourself up gradually into a standing position. Circle your shoulders front and backward, then your head gently and slowly to the right and then the left, as if you were drawing a large circle. Screw your face up like a piece of paper ready to throw in the bin – then smooth it out slowly until flat.* At first, it is easy to lose balance during the stretching sequence, but practice makes perfect. This is a wonderful exercise to learn body control and relaxed movements.

Table 4.1 Elements of voice production and variation

Voice production	Voice variation
Breath – capacity	Phrasing
Breath – control	Pausing
Breath – force	Word and sentence stress
Resonance	Dramatic emphasis
Forward production	Tone quality
Projection	Pitch and tune
Articulation vigour	Volume
Articulation agility	Pace
Correct pronunciation	Rhythm

> ### TASK 4.2
>
> *HLTA 1.3 Promote positive values, attitudes and behaviour among the pupils with whom you work.*
>
> Try beginning a series of sessions, perhaps over a week, with the above exercise. Evaluate change in focus and motivation.

Breath capacity, control and force

For normal conversation, a child's instinctive breathing is adequate. As the radius of speech extends, everyday breathing becomes insufficient. To carry voices and sustain volume over distance in a large space, a greater breath capacity and control are necessary.

However, it is important not to make children self-conscious about breathing, as they will hunch shoulders, and breathe in earnestly through their noses as if life depended on it! Such practice does more harm than good.

In conversation, we breathe through a slightly opened mouth as well as through the nose. The reason is, we have to take in air speedily. Therefore, it is not helpful to demand nose breathing in practice, as tension results from lip clamping and shoulder raising.

You can get children to understand their need for greater breath capacity by imagining that their lungs are like balloons that are normally only partly inflated, but, for speaking in a large class, need to be fully blown up. It is better to concentrate on outgoing rather than incoming air, with two aims:

1. control of *quantity* for adjustment of air to suit the length of utterance
2. control of *force* to project the voice over distance or vary energy.

> ### TASK 4.3
>
> *HLTA 3.3.1 Using clearly structured teaching and learning activities, interest and motivate pupils, and advance their learning.*
>
> Several exercises follow. Try these yourself first. Once comfortable with the introductory exercises, plan several short sessions where you introduce them to children, explaining the aims and making them fun. Monitor progression over a period of weeks.

Control of quantity

Make the snake sound **S**, by tightening the lips in a smile with the tongue tip raised behind the top teeth.

1. Say **S** in a continuous stream for 1, then 2, then 3, then 4, then 5 seconds
2. Say a long **S** letting out the breath in one continuous sound **S**_____ in two sounds of equal length, **S**_____ **S**_____ and then in 3, 4 and 5 strips.

3. Say each of the following sentences in one breath, increasing it for each sentence: *One by one and two by two the girls and boys went into the zoo. One by one, two by two, and three by three, the girls and boys skipped round the tree. One by one, two by two, three by three, and four by four the girls and boys bolted out of the door.*

Sentences should be said in chorus (perhaps three groups for the three sections) and spoken intelligently, and not gabbled in monotone. If children parrot the words, changing the background brings meaning back. Ask them to imagine an audience of animals who are watching how well boys and girls walk on two legs!

Control of force

Breath force affects the strength of sound articulation and assists the projection of voice, depending on:

1. pressure from the diaphragm – a large, flat, muscular structure under the lungs that helps to expel the air strongly from them
2. the vigorous use of lips
3. the point to which the breath is directed.

The following will help:

1. Imagine a leaf/feather on your hand, and use just enough force to blow it off.
2. Blow out an imaginary candle flame: 5, 10, 20, 30 and 40 cm away.
3. Imagine you are pumping up the tyres on a bicycle *f*_____*f*_____
   *s*_____ *s*_____ *s*_____ *S*_____ *sh*_____ *sh*_____
   *SH*_____ *SH*_____ .

Try this rhyme in a boy-girl chorus – changing roles on repetition:

Girls: This is the way we pump our tyres.

Boys: ffffffffffffff   ffffffffffffffffffff.

Girls: See them get higher and higher and higher.

Boys: ffffffffffffffffffffffff   FFFFFFFFFFFFFFFFF.

Girls: Oh dear! we've a puncture making us slower.

Boys: f==f==f==f==f==f==f==f.

Girls: See the tyres get lower and lower.

Boys: f========f==========f============f====(trailing away).

Resonance and forward projection

After the breath is set in motion, the next stage happens in the voice box (larynx) in the middle of the neck. The tone is produced here by the vibration of two hanging folds of membrane – the vocal cords. Their use is instinctive, and it is best not to draw attention to the process, as the result may be talk in the throat instead of the mouth! Focus needs to be on the third stage of this operation – *the use of resonance*.

Resonance enlarges the basic tone and takes place in hollow cavities in the skull called resonators. With a cold these become bunged up with mucus, giving voices a muffled sound. The cavities are the front of the mouth, cheekbones and forehead. Sound waves set in motion by the air pushing through the vocal cords are collected in the frontal cavities giving tone a rich fullness and pleasant rounded quality. There are two types of resonance, oral and nasal.

Oral resonance

Oral resonance involves the mouth chamber, which is rather like a cave with the soft tongue as the floor and the bony roof (hard palate) falling back into the pendulum (uvula) of the soft palate. The breath carries the sound waves into the cave, depending on:

1. room in the mouth cavity for the tone to resound
2. back and front mouth entrances wide enough for the sound easily to enter and exit.

Oral resonance is impossible if the lips and lower jaw are immobile, and exercises increase and extend activity. First, open the mouth and with fingers find the dip each side below the ear. Rub vigorously to relax the upper and lower jaws. These are hinges at the side of the face, and freeing them is like giving them a spot of oil!

1. Think of when you have been to the doctor for a sore throat and are asked to say '*Ah*' to reveal the inside of your mouth easily. Say '*Ah*' again, making the opening as big as you can. Repeat '*Ah*' several times at different speeds.
2. You have had a busy day and begin to yawn with your jaw dropped as low as it can be. Repeat in a group: *Let's yawn and yawn and yawn again ... excuse us but we're very tired!* Now try to yawn with lips closed.
3. Imagine you are a ventriloquist's doll, and your string has been pulled for your jaw to drop. Repeat several times.
4. You are at an apple-bobbing party! Reach to grab the apple from the string above your head. Bite and crunch away until every little bit is eaten!
5. How many words rhyme with jaw? *Door, floor, more, caw, saw, paw*: Make up a silly sentence like this: *I saw the cat's paw, stroking the floor, behind the door. The jackdaw says 'caw, caw' for more, torn straw*.

Nasal resonance

Nasal resonance is the enlargement of tone in the nasal cavity and hollows above the mouth as the sound waves reach them. In three English speech sounds, *m*, *n* and *ng*, the soft palate (the floppy pendulum at the end of the mouth's hard palate called the uvula) lowers to allow the breath to pass through the nose. Therefore, these consonants have greater nasal resonance than the rest, which are made with the nose cavity cut off by raising the soft palate.

The nasal sounds are used as a basis for resonance exercises. First, get children to cup their hands over their mouths and hum to a space on the wall. This gives them a sense of what resonance is. Proceed with the following:

1. You are eating a red strawberry in the sun, and the bees are humming. As you open your mouth to take another bite, a bee buzzes in too. It's inside your closed lips trying to escape – *mmmmmmmm*. It's angry and distressed – *MMMMMMMMMMM* (louder hum). Can you feel the tingle behind your teeth? (*If the children are humming in their throats, take the pitch of the note up a notch to encourage a more forward sound*).
2. Let boys and girls take alternate lines:

    Girls: *Hummmmmmmm* goes the bee as he flies around me.

    Boys: *Yummmmmmmm* goes the bee as he spies the tea.

    Girls: *Thummmmmmm* goes the bee as he gets a smack.

    Boys: *Bummmmmmmm* goes the bee as he falls on his back.

3. Encourage words with *ng* endings such as *bling, ding, fling, ting, ping, ring, sing, wing,* and *zing*, and go around the class with each child repeating an *ing* word. Imitate church bells on four different pitches with four class groups:

    Light girls' voices: *ting*.

    Dark girls' voices: *ding*.

    Light boys' voices: *kong*.

    Dark boys' voices: *gong*.

    Spoken normally, words fall in a naturally descending scale because *t* and *d* are sounds made in the same way, but the latter has voice just as in *k* and *g*. See Appendix 4.1 for voiced and voiceless consonant sounds.

Forward production

Resonance brings the voice forward in the mouth and away from the throat, thus helping carry sound over distance. The process is encouraged by practising frontal consonant sounds, as in the following examples:

- tyre pumping: *f-f-f-f-f-f-*
- tap dripping: *dr-dr-dr-dr-dr*

- baby soothing: *sh-sh-sh-sh-sh*
- snake hissing: *s-s-s-s-s-s-s-s*
- knife sharpening: *z-z-z-z-z-z-z-z*
- water hosing: *zh-zh-zh-zh-zh-zh*
- dog calling: *woof-woof-woof-woof*.

Projection

Carrying power allows voice to reach a listener without strain or shouting, depending on technical and psychological factors.

First, the speaker must know where he is sending his voice (the sound line). Always make a child aware of whom he is addressing, and if it is the whole class, this will be established through eye contact and regular eye reference. Make sure he understands that the voice has to reach everyone. Imagine the voice as a ball, which has to be thrown. To fling it over bigger distances needs practice!

Remind the audience of their responsibility, because if they listen with only half an ear, the speaker loses incentive to project voice. It is the listener-in-authority who has to put the speaker at ease before words can be delivered confidently.

Tell the story of what happened in Persia (now Iran) before telephones were invented.

> *Can you imagine a time without phones? Many years ago before we were born, the children in Persia had a way to send messages to their friends. They lived in flat-roofed houses, as it is dry there with no problems about draining water. At sundown, when light faded, children climbed the outdoor staircases to the house roofs, cupped hands and shouted a message to friends in nearby homes.*

Try this by asking for four volunteers to stand in the corners of the classroom. Give one a message such as *Meet me in the Tick Tock Club at half-past six*. He cups his hands, and looks at his friend in the corner opposite, relaying the message round until it returns. The class observes how voice changes when travelling over distance, and discuss their observations, such as that the voice is louder and slower, and words are said more clearly with greater exaggeration of movements. Moreover, the speaker fixes the listener closely and cups his hands to project the sound. All love this experience, and it is a real eye-opener, as they have never thought about this phenomenon before. It exposes them to issues involved in public speaking and assures them that is fine to talk differently in a large space. Try these exercises:

1. Say the following sentence all together, *Have you heard what's happened to Ben?*, in the following ways: *as in normal conversation; talking on the telephone; telling it as a secret to a friend; shouting it to someone 20 metres away; calling along a corridor; calling across the street; calling down a long tunnel; calling up to a sixth-floor flat from the street; calling from one hilltop to another*.
2. We are all on the shore and calling across the lake to a man dozing on his oars to let him know his boat is drifting: *Mr Miles!; Mr Miles!* (farther away);

Mr Miles! (farther still)*; Mr Miles, your boat is drifting*! If the children shout, encourage them to hum on *m* before saying the sentence. The class then invents a similar incident.

3. Put children in pairs and give a situation (prepared on cards): *a boy up a tree describes the cat he is just about to rescue; a waiter gives an order to the chef up the lift shaft; a workman on the roof shouts his requirements for lunch to a colleague at street level who is off to the shops; a man at the top of a ladder painting a window gives instructions to his wife at the bottom to go and get some more undercoat, as he is about to run out; a teacher at the top of the corridor gives instructions about the alteration in bus routines for relaying to the class.*

4. Make up a poem based on questions about a topic for two groups – the ones who *ask* and the others who *answer*. This one is called 'Dial Up'

Group 1= **1**, group 2 = **2**, etc.

1. Hello, good day! – Does rain in Spain fall mainly on the plain?
2. Yes, indeed, just as males in Wales tell funny tales.
3. Hello, hello – Do ponies in France, prance and dance?
4. They do – just like police from Nice when they go to Greece.

Language

Following on from sound awareness work, use this focus to develop sentence patterns. Further exercises in Appendix 4.1 strengthen lip, tongue and soft-palate movement for better articulation. The following diagram highlights the precise movements required in being aware of the manner and place of articulation.

Some consonant places of articulation

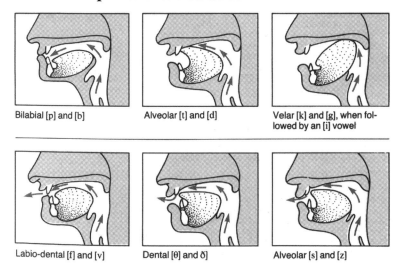

Bilabial [p] and [b]   Alveolar [t] and [d]   Velar [k] and [g], when followed by an [i] vowel

Labio-dental [f] and [v]   Dental [θ] and ð]   Alveolar [s] and [z]

Figure 4.1 Shows the mouth in cross-section and its main parts.

The following game is popular. Ask for eight volunteers. After demonstration, the class can be grouped to devise their version.

1. Give the eight children a sound name from the plosive group. Plosives are consonants where there is a complete stoppage of the air by one of the articulators, *p* and *b* – lip closure; *t* and *d* – tongue tip on the alveolar ridge behind the front teeth; *k* and *g* – back of the tongue to the back of the hard palate.
2. Get them to repeat their sounds so they have them firmly in mind – make sure the voiceless *p* is differentiated from the voiced *b*, (also *t* and *d* and *k* and *g*) by giving it just whisper and no 'er' on the end! This is a good opportunity to make the children aware of the fact that consonants come in pairs (see list in Appendix 4.1). They are made the same way but contrasted by whisper or voice. This is an important aspect to teach, as children often are confused in spelling because the voiceless sounds are always given an 'er' on the end when isolated by an adult for attention. The sounds '*p* + er' and *b* are acoustically the same, and those with problems in hearing will find it difficult to grasp the contrast for accurate use in spelling.
3. The game is played by the leader calling out a sequence of sounds, as in *t –g– b*, which can be two or more, and the children have to change places. This is a good listening opportunity.
4. After the game, ask children to nominate a sound and find words that all begin with this, as in the following instructions:
   - Think of a boy's name beginning with *b* (Billy); something he does (bounces); something he bounces (balls); a word to describe Billy (*boisterous*); a word to describe balls (*beautiful*). You now have a simple sentence with a subject (*Billy*), verb (*bounces*), object (*balls*) and descriptive words, which help visualisation of the images.
   - Point out that this is how a sentence is made and can be extended with a clause (e.g. 'Boisterous Billy, who bats for the Beacons, bounces balls beautifully'). The sentence can be as silly as you like, to make it memorable. Play a game with it.
   - Ask the group to use hands to beat the rhythm of the sentence on their thighs. Repeat it to lock it in the mind. Then start the game: Repeat the sentence with the beats, starting quietly and slowly, and each time you say it getting louder and quicker. This activity is a great release and helps the group focus on sentence patterns and their construction.

Pronunciation

Children acquire speech within the home by hearing and imitating others around them. If children are lucky, adults will coach attempts, so that clarity is encouraged from the word go! Parents will be influenced by upbringing and environment, and use sounds and words that are their norm. The particular forms of regions are known as dialects, which may vary in sounds, words and sentence structure from standard English. For example, when living in the Nottinghamshire Wolds, I heard people talk about going to *mash* – not mashing potatoes but making tea. Another expression that foxed me was *I'll go on the gas*, which meant a walk on the pavement! Sounds also are affected. In the south of England, everyone says *grass* with an open 'ah' sound, but in the North the vowel is completely flattened and sounds more like the *a* as in *cat*. As we move around various regions, we absorb some of the local characteristics, and after I had lived in the Midlands for a while, my vowels became much more centralised than they were. I do not say *cup*, as I once did, but a version that sounds more like *cerp*.

TASK 4.4

HLTA 1.1 Have high expectations of all pupils; respect their social, cultural, linguistic, religious and ethnic backgrounds, and be committed to raising their educational achievement

Try asking children if they know some words that people say differently. Discuss accents, appreciating and valuing variations while encouraging clarity.

We have many regional language forms, which differ greatly; the dialects of Bedworth, Newcastle and Glasgow are like a foreign language to me. Cultures have a high language – in our case, standard English with received pronunciation – and it is important that children have access to this and treat it like a second language, appropriate for more formal situations. This idea was frowned upon in the 1970s and regarded as elitism, but whoever heard a High Court judge speak in a strong Cockney or Birmingham accent! In certain professions, standard English is expected, and we will prevent children's possible access to them if we do not allow such language use. It is not elitism but common sense, because if we do not speak a standard form when we communicate with people from other regions or countries, they will have immense difficulty understanding us. Foreigners will have been taught this form of English, and exchange is so much easier if we can readily switch to this for the purpose of making contact with them. One of the competences of an effective communicator is appropriateness of the form, content and use of language for the occasion; therefore, learning both high and low (dialectal) English is important.

In school, the child receives the more deliberate attempt of an adult, who will probably change some of the sounds (at least while in school), towards either standard English or a modification of local accent. This process goes on to a greater or lesser extent throughout schooling, depending on the knowledge, views and values of staff. Children from homes using an approximation to standard English are likely to have less difficulty in learning to read and write because their normal talk more closely resembles printed English, at least in syntax and vocabulary. Other pupils will face more problems and need support.

Attitude is very important with regard to the issue of language forms. We have to clear our minds of the notion that one type of pronunciation is better than another because it is the one we happen to use. Such a belief dies hard and leaves behind a mass of unconscious prejudices. A dialect is a legitimate form of English, and it has been claimed that West Country speech would be our present standard if the King's court had remained in Winchester and not moved to London! Now, standard English is based on the Home Counties style – the areas that surround our capital. We have to review and perhaps revise any right–wrong attitude toward dialect features. Children will sense it if we regard their home language as inferior. Their instinct will be to defend parents' language. Thus, educators need to find ways to show respect for dialects that are different from their own. Discussing the meaning of local words and comparing them with standard ones is not only fascinating but also important in helping children understand language differences.

TASK 4.5

HLTA 1.1 Have high expectations of all pupils; respect their social, cultural, linguistic, religious and ethnic backgrounds, and be committed to raising their educational achievement

Now try asking children whether they know words that mean the same thing – give some examples from your locality. Discuss dialect, noting the difference from accent, and appreciating and valuing variations while encouraging clarity.

This does not deny the importance of technical work on speech. Pronunciation is only one dimension of speaking. Behind it is *voice* and articulation in words – and if this is dead and slovenly, the impression of a person will be negative. Whether children use dialect or standard pronunciation, or something between, they can learn to speak it well, but if it has no value for them, they learn to speak it indifferently.

Educators are often overwhelmed by the 45 different speech sounds (see the tables in Appendix 4.1) and think they have to be dealt with separately. They get out a phonetics textbook, which completely baffles them, and decide to abandon the whole business of teaching children to speak. There is, however, another way, which is to focus on two basic speech factors: *voice and articulation*, rather than on individual speech sounds.

This approach will not harm a genuine dialect, and other forms of pronunciation will be improved with the minimum of effort. If we encourage children to become aware of jaws, lips, tongue, soft palates and resonators, it will help cure flatness and nasality in vowels and diphthongs (sound blends). Agile lips and tongues used with vigour will make consonants firm and clear. Let us now consider the most important vowel.

The neutral vowel

Although the neutral vowel is only one of the 45 sounds of English, it is of such importance that it deserves individual treatment. The vowel is the little one, known as a *schwa* and written as an inverted *e*. You find it at the beginning of words such as 'among' and at the end of 'china'. It is not the same sound as *u* in *but*, although it sounds similar. We need awareness of its use in many words despite their spelling: *breakfast, brother, burden, comfort, cupboard, garden, hundred, mother, pupil, spoken*.

What do you notice about this list? The neutral vowel occurs only in unstressed syllables. In teaching children, we respect the conventions of normal, educated people and do not encourage unnatural pronunciations. Clarity depends on the effective articulation of a phrase, and not on the over-pronunciation of a single word. Children need to understand that words influence others in a sequence. Take the word 'cat' and let us see the effect of surrounding words – *The cat is on the mat* is said *The cat's on the mat.* In the sentence, *The cat and dog are friendly*, we say, *The ca? n 'dog....*' In the first case, the vowel *i* is elided to help the fluency, and the *t* is weak. In the second, the *t* is replaced by a glottal sound made by the glottis (fleshy part of the air passage in the throat), which opens and closes instead of the tongue tip making closure with the alveolar ridge behind the top teeth. At the same time, the *a* and *d* of the word *and* are elided to make the sequence flow. This makes us realise that speaking is a great deal more complicated than we think.

The use of the neutral vowel is carried still further, as, apart from the words that include it, there are others that change in connected speech: *a, and, as, but, can, for, from, of, the, to, was et, at .*

The words – *the, a* and *to* are said as *thee, ay* and *too* in isolation, but in connected speech their dictionary vowel is replaced by a neutral one in phrases such as:

- *a new coat*
- *salt and pepper*
- *come as quickly as you can*
- *see you at 3 o'clock*
- *not only but also*
- *I can do it*
- *I bought it for 10 pence*
- *they came from Leicester*
- *one of the best books*
- *the* girl is here* (*the* becomes *thi* before another vowel – *the elegant girl*)
- *she came to* work* (may use u as in *put*)
- *where was she found?*

To say these words as in isolation would prevent the listener from picking up the vital ones, as we neutralise the vowels in the less important to speed them up and emphasise those that carry meaning. Once children have grasped the neutral vowel, they will be much more aware of the information-carrying words in a sentence and be able to catch meaning much quicker than before. Try it and see!

Phrasing

We do not speak in words but in groups known as phrases. If I say to my husband (as he appears with a welcome cup of tea) *I – think – it – might – rain*, in response to the dark clouds outside, he will have difficulty making the thought complete. In speech, we automatically take in enough breath to say the phrase and send it out on a continuous stream of air in which words are threaded like beads on a necklace. The word clusters in a sentence are the units of speech. This is important because, as educators, we tend to give individual words attention in vocabulary lists, spelling tests and dictionaries. There is a tendency to reduce the whole to parts, and it is important to treat the business of speaking in its reality, and then we will have more understanding of the communicative process and less problems in its use. There are two aims in helping children develop talk:

1. grouping of words so that listeners immediately catch the sense.
2. adapting phrase lengths in verse and prose speaking or reading.

Exercises develop those things already considered in breath control, and each sentence should be said in a single breath. Take a new breath at the end of each one.

1. *It was cold.* (repeat twice).
2. *It was cold when I went outside* (repeat twice).
3. *It was cold when I went outside to find my ball* (repeat twice). Stress and pronounce as normal: *It w'z cold*, and not *It woz cold*.

The application of exercises to reading is important. When reading, the eye dashes ahead of the voice to assess the next phrase and decide which words must be joined together to form sense groups. Comprehension and intelligible reading depend most on phrase recognition.

TASK 4.6

HLTA 3.2.3 Monitor pupils' participation and progress, providing feedback to teachers, and giving constructive support to pupils as they learn.

Help children work on a piece of their own text as follows:

Ben was late for football practice. Why? Because he stopped off to get himself a chocolate bar. And what do you think happened? 'Ben, this is the second time you've been late,' said Mr Green, the coach. 'You will be left out of this week's match.' Oh dear! Chocolate does not make up for losing the chance to beat the Liver Boys!

Studying phrasing in a reading passage helps children who find the process difficult, by showing them the structure for making meaning. You mark phrases with a stroke or copy them on separate lines to show how they vary in length:

Ben was late for football practice.

Why?

Because he stopped off to get himself a chocolate bar.

And what do you think happened?

'Ben, this is the second time you've been late,'

said Mr Green, the coach.

'You will be left out of this week's match'.

Oh dear!

Chocolate does not make up for losing the chance to beat the Liver Boys!

Children who find listening to others or reading texts difficult can benefit from a session where they have to copy out a short passage in phrase format. They are then able to see phrases as meaningful units and are not confused by a jumble of words that they cannot sort out. In speaking verse, the need for correct phrasing is vital because the music, as well as the meaning of the words, depends on it. The tendency is to take a breath at the end of a line:

Slowly, silently, the blue balloon /

Floats through the sky like the midnight moon. /

An interpretation that makes sense would be:

Slowly,/ silently,/ the blue balloon

Floats through the sky/ like the midnight moon.

The phrases flow from one stroke to the next, but there is a **hold** not a **breath** at the run-on word *balloon*, so that the couplet does not turn into prose. One should not go so overboard on phrase work that the enjoyment of a story or poem is destroyed, but demonstrating this way to make meaning, greatly enhances the chances of children processing and producing effective spoken and written communication.

Pausing

There is an alternating pattern of phrase, pause, phrase, in a piece of talk or text. The pause has several functions:

- It enables a speaker to take breath for the next phrase.
- It gives the listener time to take in what is said.
- It gives the speaker time to decide what to say next.

In reading aloud and interpreting other people's words, the pause is essential to give time to look ahead and collect the words for the next phrase. Generally, however, children take a breath, read on until it is finished, snatch another one, probably midphrase, and so on. Although nerves may play a part, this performance is mainly due to the fact that pupils are tuned into accurate word recognition above all else. We have to persuade people that writing is speech on paper, and when reading aloud, you have to put the words into speech again. The more we link spoken and written activities, the better the result, as phrasing will become natural and the passage easier to grasp. The power of visualising and imagining are important aids:

> *The boy lifted the ball. / He aimed. / He flung it at the wicket. / The batsman was out. Cheers echoed over the field.*

Without the pauses marked by the strokes, the reading is ineffective. The reader has to be taught to see the things he is describing. He will then pause naturally, and the listener will be able to see them too. As well as seeing and understanding, the pause helps the listener to feel what is happening.

> *Red Riding Hood was walking through the wood. / She lost her way. / It began to get dark and damp. / She decided to lie down under a tree and fell asleep. / Not long after, a wolf sauntered by./ He stopped at seeing Red Riding Hood. / / He crouched and waited. / / / Then, with a growl, he pounced.*

By encouraging the child to feel what is happening, the pauses are made instinctively and differently in length. As the drama of the event builds up, so the pause increases. This is so much better than saying to the child: *Well, after 'Hood,' pause to a count of two, and after 'waited,' to the count of three!*

Pauses may take on other purposes. They give time for audience reactions and allow speakers to express themselves through other means such as facial expression and gesture. They also point up a dramatic situation. The dramatic pause builds atmosphere: *Tom stood near the / entrance.* Pausing briefly before *entrance* signals the importance of the word within the narrative.

Stressing

Words of two or more syllables have one that is stressed: *A'nother, be'cause, co'mmand, de'cide, 'ea/ger, 'fall/en, 'gall/op, im'possible.*

Similarly, in speech, some words have more stress than others because of their importance in the sentence meaning: *'Give me the 'other book.*

These stressed words are known as content words, as they carry the basic meaning: *give* and *other*. In real contexts, the stressing comes naturally with the feeling of the situation, but this has to be imagined in abstract ones. The purpose of stressing is to simplify the message to save the listener the trouble of sorting out values for himself. We are intimating, therefore, that these are the words that hold the meaning, so take notice! Too much stressing of words makes the task of deciphering the gist more difficult.

TASK 4.7

HLTA 3.2.3 Monitor pupils' participation and progress, providing feedback to teach-ers, and giving constructive support to pupils as they learn.

1. Help children identify the content words in the following sentences:

    He is catching the bus to the football ground.

    I am getting a new Game Boy tomorrow.

    Would you like a strawberry ice cream?

    Stop that noise. I'm trying to listen to my new DVD.

2. Act out the content words

    This extends the last activity. The class picks out the content words and then says the sentence with natural stressing while a chosen child acts it out.

    She walked to the cupboard and chose a book.

    He crept to the window and peeped out.

    She ambled to the door and opened it silently.

    He went to the whiteboard and drew a large house.

Emphasis

Until now, we have been concerned with selecting words in ordinary state-ments or questions. In emphatic speech, we are more selective. We reduce the number of stressed words but give them greater prominence. It marks the dif-ference between: *I love 'chicken curry* and *I 'love chicken curry*. Additional feeling is often the reason for special emphasis, but it often marks contrast: *For want of a good batsman, the 'match was lost.*

Or emphasis may mean that the words imply a deeper meaning. *She **says** she did her homework*, indicates the speaker holds a different view. In the fol-lowing sentences emphasise each word in turn and ask the class to discuss the implication, eg *I don't know*.

> ***I** don't know (someone else might) I **don't** know (denial). I don't **know** (I'll guess).*

- *Where do you think he is?*
- *I want blue shoes, not red.*
- *I need £5 to buy that book.*
- *Is that a rabbit on the lawn?*

The fact that meaning can be altered without changing words intrigues children!

TASK 4.8

HLTA 3.2.2 Monitor pupils' responses to learning tasks and modify their approach accordingly.

Try this with children and see whether they can explain the difference in meanings Take the sentence, *I love chocolate*, and try emphasising each word to see how meaning changes.

1. *I* love chocolate (I – not any old Tom, Dick and Harry!).

2. I *love* chocolate (not indifferent, even mildly liking or vehemently hating – but a strong, passionate, positive feeling!).

3. I love *chocolate* (not cheese or chutney).

Then explore a selection of the activities recommended below with children after trying them yourself first.

Pitch and tune

Pitch

There are three main pitch differences, high, medium and low, and children need to understand these in a meaningful way in a story:

1. Tell the story of *The Three Bears*, using a low pitch for father bear, a medium for mother and a high one for baby. Children love the three different ways of saying: *Who's been eating my porridge?*
2. Give the children three contrasting characters: an elephant, monkey and a fly and ask them to make up a dialogue around an incident, with different pitches for the characters.
3. Make the sound of these different-size bells: little silver bell – *ting*; school bell – *ding*; large church bell – *dong*.
4. Ask the class to make up sounds for the following: bicycle bell (*ting-a-ling*); car horn (*beep, beep*); trumpet (*ta, ta, ta, ta*); flute (*tootle toot, tootle toot*); bus horn (*bong, bong*).

Tune (intonation)

The ideal voice is one that uses the whole range of natural pitches. Humorous verse makes good practice material because it depends on using a variety of intonation to make the point. The following exercises are useful.

The adult puts the following questions, and children answer with *m* – changing the inflection to suit.

1. *Do you like fish and chips?*
2. *Do you like rats?*
3. *Would you like to win the lottery?*
4. *Do you think you'll ever visit the moon?*

Try this choral activity: with three individual speakers and a class chorus:

> All: *Rrrrrrrrrrrrrrrrrrrrrrr* (low).
> 1. *The engine roars so close the doors!*
>   All: *Weeeeeeeeeeeee* (medium).
> 2. *The plane weaves over the trees!*
>   All: *Mmmmmmmmmm* (high).
> 3. *The plane hums and down it comes!*
>   All: *Wooooooooo* (high-low).

Gabby Gossip

1. *Gabby Gossip got a goat and goldfish.*
2. *Did Gabby Gossip get a goat and goldfish?*
3. *If Gabby Gossip got a goat and goldfish, where's the goat and goldfish that Gabby Gossip got?*

Lastly, try a nonsense story for eight speakers:

1. *Mickey Mouse popped out to the garden to cut a lettuce to wash his hair.*
2. *Just then, the Jumblies stopped at the fish and chop shop.*
3. *What! No fish food?*
4. *So they jumped into the canal and swam down to meet the moon.*
5. *The Star Gazers were having a wedding and the Tonguewagglers attended*
6. *and the Lipwobblers…*
7. *and the Tooth Fairy, herself, swathed in furs and jewels, with a blood-red satin pillbox perched on her raven curls.*
8. *So they ended up curling until champagne ran out of their boots, and they fell as rain back to earth.*

Nonsense is so much easier to make dramatic and it encourages the use of constant pitch changes! Flatness is the deadly sin of reading aloud. The straight lines of the text induce a level pitch. Yet, witness children in the playground – the pitch-changes of pupils at play are incredible. If only we could encourage the same animation in the classroom, but this is a matter of technique and tenacity.

Written English is a second language for children and bears no connection to everyday concerns. Somehow, we must open the gate and let some life into what pupils often consider as boring, irrelevant activities. It is time to bring the fun back into teaching!

Pace

Pace is a deceiver! We chide a child for speaking fast when the fault is not in the rate but in lack of adequate pausing between phrases. If pace is slackened, impetus and rhythm can be lost. In addition to work on pausing, we can also encourage more self-awareness in the listener/s. Successful talking is both communication and expression. A child gabbles because he feels compelled to unload his word container – in an untidy heap as often as not! So make sure he has good listeners, and encourage self-expression to keep audience interest.

Pace must suit mood and meaning. A sad statement will be slow, low and measured, but a glad one, high in pitch and speed. The aim is flexibility, and pace needs to adjust to the needs of thoughts and feelings.

Try the following:

- *The grandfather clock goes TICK-TOCK, TICK-TOCK (slow).*
- *The clock on the mantelpiece goes TICK-TACK TICK-TACK (medium).*
- *The wristwatch goes TICK-A-TACKER, TICK-A-TACKER (fast).*

Change pace in the following sentences:

Slow: *I can't think where I left my cap.*
Medium: *Use your loaf, Tom. It's on your head.*
Fast: *Run for your life, Tom, or we'll miss the match!*

To sum up, speech should not be slowed for the sake of diction. Rather, we need to improve diction to match the natural requirements of speed, in line with the value of pausing. The rate of speaking should never exceed the speaker's thoughts.

Tone

Tone is the musical quality of the voice; it is produced in the larynx and enlarged in the resonators of the skull. Like a picture of self in sound, voice is one of our most distinctive and revealing features. Our basic tone – assuming the vocal apparatus is being used properly – is under the influence of mind and feelings, and is capable of infinite variation. A good voice is like a violin – responsive to the touch and technique of the user. Some children's voices, because of poor models at home and lack of attention at school, are restricted in range, and harsh in quality. The remedy lies in breath control, resonance and projection, which help to bring the voice forward and give it freedom and full-ness. Tone change, however, is the outward effect of an inward change. Exercises should not be produced in an emotional vacuum.

Try the following ideas:

1. Say the sentence: *What! No milk for my tea!* as if spoken by a sad old man; a bright, breezy teacher; an angry giant; a wicked witch; a fussy lady; a proud king.
2. Divide the children into 4-6 groups with a phrase to repeat: *hot dogs and pickle; strawberry ice cream; fish and chips with mushy peas; fruit and orange jelly; custard tarts and cream; beef curry and rice.* The children represent crowds of people, one is happy, others are excited, sad, angry, tired and droopy, and the final one is nervous and worried. The adult calls out one of the phrases, and the children move round the room saying their phrase in their crowd-mood to as many as possible.

If voices are dull, the fault is not always due to technical deficiencies. The causes may be boredom and lack of interest, limited understanding of what is required and repetition without thought, due to the mind being detached and preoccupied with other concerns. Obviously, exercises will not correct these.

Volume

If there is good voice projection and clear articulation, loudness is rarely necessary. Children will discriminate between degrees of loudness by exercises as follows:

1. *The little hammer goes tip, tip; the big one goes tap, tap; and the very large one goes BANG, BANG.*
2. Have a group of boys and girls face each other and say alternate lines:

   THE OLD FOLK

   Grandpa, Grandma, will you come a-clearing?
   Speak a little louder, dears, we're very hard of hearing.
   Grandpa, Grandma, will you come a-cleaning?
   Speak a little louder, dears, we cannot get your meaning.
   Grandpa, Grandma, will you come a-walking?
   Speak a little louder, dears, or what's the use of talking?
   Grandpa, Grandma, we all love you dearly.
   Oh! Thank you kindly, dears, we hear you very clearly.

3. Get the children to supply sentences for these occasions:
   Loud: A football match. Talking over noise on the television. A playground accident.
   Normal: Speaking on the phone. Asking for a bus ticket. Telling a friend about your new video.
   Soft: Passing a secret message. Talking while the baby is asleep. Telling your friend about a present for another friend so he cannot overhear.
4. Suggest a situation for these lines: *Get out of the room! Look out! Let me go! How dare you do that! I can't believe it! What a surprise!*

These exercises are useful in getting over the point that noise is usually less effective than energy or intensity. This comes from the force of breath, which carries the sound and from the firm articulation that shapes it.

Rhythm

This is the last but not the least dimension of vocal variation that is partly language and partly personality. Every phrase spoken has its special rhythm, which comes from the traditional pattern of English speech but is given subtle variations from the temperament and habits of the speaker. We can help pupils by:

1. making sure we respect the natural rhythms of speaking
2. encouraging freedom of expression.

The tip is not to be pedantic in speaking. For example: *Shee weent too thee shoow*, is not rhythmic or English-sounding, but *She went to the show* is both.

Try activity rhymes, as the movements help the flow of the words:

> *Row, row, row the boat, row it to the beach.*
>
> *Tie, tie, tie the boat, so it's out of reach.*

Older children can compare the rhythms of different poems that are on the same theme to become aware of different compositions. Rhythm is a vital part of understanding poetry. Verse heightens everyday speech, and the intensity of the rhythm gives shape and form. But poetic rhythms are based on those of normal speech. The distinctive metre/beat pattern is the scaffolding on which the rhythm is built. Although many consider that rhymes are old-fashioned, such a view does not take into account the importance of verse in building vocabulary, sound and sentence patterns. Rhymes also allow us to practise speech techniques and become aware of what is involved in building the meaning of messages.

Summary

Technique is a subject covering many related abilities. It deserves value and respect, such as that attributed to the technical side of other activities like music and sport. We regard exercise and practice as essential for most movements, but, surprisingly, we neglect this when it comes to our most important physical, mental and emotional activity – communication. Because the complexity of speech and children's potential for using it are forgotten, we pay it superficial attention.

The purpose of speech is the expression of thought and feeling, but its communication depends on both physical and mental control. This is true of both spontaneous speaking and more formal oral activities. Success in anything requires the mastery of technique, and this is never achieved with out dedication and devotion.

Key Points

- Introducing direct speech work in schools demands that we view it as an important underpinning to all learning, and not merely a waste of class time.
- Valuing speech techniques allows children to become aware of the vocal dynamics marking meaning, and their practice enhances comprehension.
- Speech technique is the bridge between speaker and listener, but we do not give it the respect and attention that is accorded to technique in other activities.
- Speaking involves both voice production and variation, and these need training.
- Speech techniques are easy to introduce into 5–10-minute slots and can be part of all lesson plans.
- There is no gift like the gift of speech, and the level at which we learn to use it is the level at which we live our lives.

How Can You Help Children with Communication Difficulties?

This chapter:

- considers some of the particular problems in communicating that hamper personal and academic progress, including
  - physical and psychological causes
  - bad habits
  - having to cope with English as a second language to the one spoken at home
- suggests how understanding of problems can help pupils overcome difficulties
- offers strategies that can be employed to help improve situations so that children can participate and be included in curriculum activities.

Problems in communicating

The problems cover a wide range of factors from minor speech articulation problems to severe sensory impairments of hearing, sight, movement and feeling that reduce information–processing capacity. Communication development depends on intact senses, motor abilities, intelligence and a social environment in which emotional needs are nourished. Communication is impaired when it deviates so far from the behaviour of others that it calls attention to itself, interfering with interaction, and causing learning and behaviour disturbances. The categories are as follows:

1. physical
2. psychological
3. bad habits
4. English as a second language.

TASK 5.1

HLTA 1.7 Be aware of the statutory frameworks relevant to your role.

Consider the four principles below (Disability Equality in Education at **www.diseed.org.uk**) and prepare comments on each as you read through this chapter. Use comments and examples to debate inclusion with colleagues. Is yours a truly inclusive environment?

- Disabled children and those with learning difficulties belong and have a right to the support they need in ordinary classes.

- All children with and without impairments benefit from inclusion, which is an important component of a quality education.

- All children have a right to an education that will prepare them for life in the community.

- The kinds of teaching and learning which are good for inclusion are good for all children.

Physical causes

These problems range from structural malformations of the oral cavity to sensory losses affecting information-processing capacity, such as hearing and visual losses, and neurological deficits that affect speech and writing (dyslexia).

Oral malformations

Cleft lip and palate, enlarged adenoids, and misalignment of jaws, teeth or tongue all interfere with clear speaking. Many require surgical treatment over long periods. For example, in cleft lip and palate, repairs start soon after birth, but if the malformation is extensive there will be several operations during growth. Similarly, jaw misalignments and abnormal bite positions require long-term orthodontics, but often not until the child has finished skull growth, posing particular problems for saying sounds accurately. After operations, help may be needed to change established speaking patterns. School staff can cooperate in guiding a child toward normal speech and communication.

Other physical troubles are not so visible. A child may have an unusually hoarse voice, which does not go away, and this could be due to chronic laryngitis, catarrh or a vocal cord defect known as singer's nodes/vocal nodules. These are granular bumps that interfere with the smooth motion of the vocal cords as they adduct (come together) and abduct (move apart) to make sound. Correct breathing and posture and soft attack on sounds is vital to prevent complete voice loss. Laser surgery removes persistent nodes, due to persistent vocal abuse and poor speaking techniques, and is followed by voice rest and speech re-education. Too much shouting in the playground and not enough voice projection! This is a common problem, too, among teachers, with 10 % giving up their jobs because of persistent voice loss. Again, this is the consequence of lack of attention paid to public-speaking needs.

Sometimes, a child may have a wide nasopharynx – the part of the throat visible when you look into the back of your mouth. This prevents contact between soft palate and throat, cutting off nasal passages and allowing breath to be orally expelled. The result is nasal speech, commonly associated with cleft lip/palate. Enlarged adenoids also disturb nasal resonance; a child with this condition sounds as if speaking with a cold. Such problems are often ignored, resulting in secondary psychological disturbances such as depression and disaffection. It is important to work with medical specialists to achieve potential for clear speech. The management of children with hearing problems is detailed next as a common accompaniment to other speech problems.

Hearing problems

Levinson (1988) suggests that over 90% of children with learning difficulties have a history of ear infection and a degree of deafness. It is difficult to detect hearing deficits, and the brighter the child is, the more he tends to hide the problem successfully from others. In younger children, glue ear (otitis media) involves fluid collecting in the middle ear, becoming thick and infected, and interfering with sound conduction. Children often suffer frequent bouts and live in a world of their own, as it becomes a problem to listen. As many as four out of five children have glue ear before school age (Sage, 2004), preventing them from hearing and acquiring speech accurately.

Signs of hearing loss

- inattention; appearing to hear only when he wants to; daydreaming
- talks more loudly than normal or talks less and is withdrawn
- turns up sound on TV, audio player or computer
- says *pardon*? or *what*? frequently
- fails to hear sound out of visual range
- experiences pain if suffering from glue ear
- tiredness caused by the extra attention required
- tinnitus, vertigo (cochlea linked to balance organs)
- recruitment – sensitivity to sound
- makes inappropriate comments and may be disruptive in lessons
- confuses words that sound similar (*fat, that, vat*)
- shows limited vocabulary, syntax and sound use, and finds it difficult to repeat accurately
- misinterprets information or responds to only part of it
- watches others carefully to see what they do in order to follow suit
- has frequent colds and coughs.

To understand hearing impairment, one must appreciate two features of sound measurement – level and frequency. Sound *level* is the volume of sound measured in decibels (dB). At a standard distance of 3 feet:

- whispered speech = 30 dB
- normal speech = 60 dB
- loud shouting = 90 dB.

Sound *frequency* is the main physical basis of our subjective impression of sound *pitch*. Frequency determines whether we hear sound as high or low and is measured in hertz (Hz). The lowest C on the piano is 32 Hz and the highest C is 2000 Hz (2 kHz). The normal hearing range for people is 100 – 10,000 Hz (10 kHz). Hearing can be impaired in the range of frequencies one can hear, or the volume of sound, or both. With regard to frequency, unless a person can hear within the range 500 – 2000 Hz (2 kHz) it is likely speech development is affected. This is summarised in Table 5.1.

Table 5.1 Hearing loss

Decibel loss	Impairment
0	None
1–40	Slight-mild – some difficulties understanding speech
41–70	Moderate – difficulty with normal (41–55) and loud (56–70) speech
71–90	Severe – limited understanding of speech
96 plus	Profound – rarely showing understanding of speech

Types of hearing loss

- Mono-aural loss is loss in one ear only and presenting no problems in one-to-one talk, but in large groups and big spaces, there are difficulties in discriminating and locating sounds which depend on two ears for correct processing.
- Conductive loss means impediments in the transmission of sound to the cochlear caused by wax, foreign objects or excess of middle ear fluid that has become thick and infected, causing inflammation (glue ear/otitis media).
- Sensory loss is loss caused by nerve damage before or after birth.

How do you cope with hearing problems?

Conductive loss may respond to medicines, but if it is persistent, miniature ventilation tubes (grommets) are inserted into the eardrum and stay in place for 6–12 months before falling out to allow the hole to heal. The procedure may need repeating to keep the ear drained and hearing improved.

Sensory losses cannot be restored, but aids can be fitted to make better use of residual hearing by increasing sound volume. Children are now offered cochlear implants, which offer the possibility of increased hearing. The following tips can help not only children's hearing problems but also other conditions that need attention to speech patterns to facilitate change:

- Those with mild losses must look directly at the speaker. Ambient classroom noise can be dampened down by carpets and curtains, but if this is not possible, a hearing expert can provide advice for a particular context.
- Moderate and severe losses need visual clues such as lip-reading and sign language. Radio aids can be used, the transmitter being worn by the speaker and the receiver by the child.
- Speak slowly and clearly without shouting and use supportive gestures.
- Remember children with glue ear feel under par and are listless.

Class organisation

- Attract the child's attention by calling his name before asking a question or giving an instruction and step out of the group to make focus easier.
- Do not stand with your back to the light such that your face movements are in shadow.
- Talk face to face, sitting/bending to the same level in exchanges.
- Seat the child in the front of the class to see clearly.
- Cut down background noise and provide good lighting.
- Keep instructions short and simple.
- Present one source of information at a time. It is difficult to focus on what you are saying as well as looking at a book or watching writing on a board.
- Explain the problem to classmates and suggest how they can help.
- Sound-symbol work will be a problem in the literacy hour, and the child will need the support of a TA trained to deal with hearing loss.

TASK 5.2

HLTA 1.6 Improve your own practice, through observation, evaluation and discussion with colleagues.

Discuss with colleagues experiences in working with children with hearing problems. What have they found that works? Which of the above would be sensible practice when working with all children?

Visual problems

Children with sight difficulties are handicapped in communicating because they do not have the visual context from which to gain meaning. The majority with sight problems are educated in mainstream schools, and, given support, they usually do well. In some cases, however, difficulties are not detected or understood.

Types and characteristics

Visual acuity. This is measured by the Snellen and Jaeger charts. The Snellen Chart comprises lines of letters in progressively smaller typefaces. The size of the letters on each line is designed so that it is known at what distance a person with normal sight can read that line accurately. It is calculated by the following formula:

$$\text{Visual acuity} = \frac{\text{distance from the chart}}{\text{letter size}}$$

A visual acuity of 6:36 means that a child reads letters at only 6 metres that a normal person sees at 36 metres. This ratio suggests the level at which a child will need vision aids and blind registration. The Jaeger chart assesses near vision with lines of print of different sizes and gives an indication of suitable reading material – normal print, large print books, etc.

Fields of vision. This defines limitation in the field of vision. When one looks directly forward with one eye at a time, the object that is in visual focus is seen clearly, but those around is less so. The range of what is seen without eye movement is the field of vision.

Colour vision. Defective colour vision affects education when colour is used in teaching. One in 50 is affected, mostly males, with difficulty commonly in distinguishing between red and green. The Ishihara test comprises cards with numbers or patterns in spots of contrasting colours. The patterns seen differ according to degree of normal colour vision.

Associated conditions. Malformations of the cornea, the lens or the globe of the eye may be caused by **retinitis pigmentosa**, a hereditary degenerative disease of the retina, or may be the effect of maternal rubella, or **Usher's syndrome**, a genetic condition causing progressive visual impairment and sensorineural loss. About 35% of children with severe/profound hearing loss have visual impairments.

Characteristics of visual problems

- inflamed, weepy, cloudy or bloodshot eyes
- squints and eyes not aligned and working together
- rapid, involuntary eye movements, blinking, rubbing or screwing up of eyes
- discomfort in bright light
- head held at an awkward angle or book at an unusual angle/distance
- headaches or dizziness
- clumsiness, missing the table when putting things on it, bumping into objects
- failure to respond to questions, commands or gestures unless addressed by name.

How to manage visual impairment (VI)

Some problems, such as squints, resulting from muscle imbalance, can be surgically corrected. Acuity problems are improved with prescriptive glasses. Otherwise, difficulties are managed with visual aids. It is even possible to have readers that turn written material into sound. While assessments of visual acuity, field of vision and colour vision are important, an assessment of functional vision is necessary to determine educational needs.

When it is thought that vision is impaired, educational advice must be sought from a qualified teacher of the blind according to the regulations (1983) following the Education Act 1981. Support is necessary for pupil and educators, and it includes:

- advice on teaching materials, low vision aids and illuminations from the VI service
- opportunities for pupils to get to know school and its layout
- encouragement to wear glasses if recommended and check for cleanliness.

Class organisation

- Ask a specialist teacher to advise on the condition and implications.
- Give clear information, as gestures and facial expressions are often misread.
- Use the child's name to get attention.
- Sit him at the front and near to the board, television or overhead projector.
- Allow extra time for finishing tasks.
- Provide him with his own resource materials so that he does not have to share.
- Do not stand and deliver near a window that silhouettes you.
- Keep work areas well lit with no glare. Some pupils are photophobic (sensitive to light) and more comfortable in shade.
- Present short tasks to prevent tiring.
- Draw attention to wall displays, as they may not be noticed.
- Ensure tidiness: identify personal space with pegs/lockers at the end of rows.
- Discover useful equipment such as talking scales.
- Enlarge resource texts to 16 or 18 font, using good spacing for information; avoid italics and use lower case because its ascenders and descenders give more distinctive shape. Use short lines of text and unjustified margins with paper that is matt rather than glossy.
- Avoid clutter and use strong contrasts to highlight important things.

TASK 5.3

HLTA 2.1 Have sufficient understanding of a specialist area to support pupils' learning, and be able to acquire further knowledge to contribute effectively and with confidence to the classes in which you are involved.

Evaluate the organisation of the classroom you work in against the above criteria. What changes would be needed to be made to make learning accessible to children with visual problems? What equipment is available to help?

Communication disorders: speech, language and social use (semantic-pragmatics)

Communication problems affect understanding and using verbal and non-verbal forms as well as moving muscles for speaking. Around 10% of children have bad deficits. The causes may be genetic flaws, biological disturbances such as hearing loss or cleft palate, injury, illness, general learning difficulties and lack of opportunity or stimulation.

Aspects and characteristics

- **The speech apparatus** includes the mouth, tongue, lips, nose, and muscles. Incorrect or inefficient functioning leads to impairments such as dysfluency (stammering).
- **Phonology** refers to the sounds that make up language, and problems occur in the wrong use of vowels and consonants.
- **Grammar** refers to word function such as that of nouns, verbs, adjectives, adverbs, conjunctions and connectives, and problems are exhibited in the selection of the wrong form (e.g. *I runny* for *I am running* – an adjectival form used instead of a verb one).
- **Syntax** is the way words and sentences are put together in conventional subject – verb–object relationships (e.g. *I* [subject] *went running* [verb] *in the mountains* [object]. Difficulties are evident in the muddled use of these patterns (e.g. *Running I mountains went*).
- **Semantics** refers to word meanings. The most common 500 words have approximately 15,000 different meanings (e.g. *run*). Problems are common in maths when children do not grasp that everyday phrases (e.g. *take away*) have another use in numerical calculations.
- **Pragmatics** refers to how verbal and non-verbal language is used to express feelings and ideas in different contexts. Problems occur with inappropriate use for a situation because clues and nuances of the exchange are not noticed and understood. Because this involves thinking ability, such children cannot cope with abstract words such as *imagine, guess*, and *next*, and they often appear stupid, rude, arrogant, gauche and oversensitive or insensitive to situations.
- **Prosody** refers to the intonation and stress (rhythm) of speech. Problems are seen in the poor use of vocal dynamics – pitch, pace, pause, power and pronunciation – speech commonly being too fast or slow, and monotonous in tone. As we mark meaning with these dynamics, their lack of use in our own speech is reflected in poor understanding of others.

Management

Children have two broad categories of difficulty:

- **receptive** – understanding the meaning of what others say and do
- **expressive** – using words, gestures (including eye contact and reference), movements, facial expressions, voice tone and social conventions so that others can understand what you say and do.

Problems across the range may be considered within the autistic spectrum disorders, as children will have difficulty in processing all the information from a situation and responding appropriately. Children with specific problems or delay will need advice/input from a therapist and the support in school of the COGS. Do not expect spontaneous or generalised learning. These children are hard work but rewarding.

As education centres on communication, any impairment will affect cognitive, emotional and social abilities. Assessment of communication needs a clear, structural model such as categories of reception and expression. Difficulties may also be structured according to mode of transmission – speech, print or gesture (including sign language). An example of speech impairment is a stammer, a disorder involving print is dyslexia, and dyspraxia demonstrates a problem in carrying out a pattern of movement, despite the person understanding what is required and being physically able to comply. An aspect of dyspraxia may be deficits in speech coordination, in which sounds can be made but not sufficiently controlled to form words.

Another classification of disorders is *organic* and *functional*. Organic problems have an explicit medical cause, such as aphasia caused by damage/abnormality to the cerebral cortex. Receptive aphasia is lack of understanding; expressive aphasia is inability to form ideas and put them into words. Functional disorders have no clear medical cause and include some examples of dyslexia where no brain abnormalities are demonstrated. Another distinction is between *delay* and *deviance*. Delay refers to a normal pattern, which is slow to develop, whereas deviance signifies abnormal growth features.

TASK 5.4

HLTA 2.9 Know a range of strategies to establish a purposeful learning environment.

Try some of these tips within your practice:

- Use short sentences with good pauses between them to give time for processing (e.g. *Put books and pencils in your work trays* rather than *Tidy up*.

- Always check for understanding and define unfamiliar words.

- Supplement speech with appropriate gestures, movements and visual props.

- Make voice expressive and interesting to listen to.

- Give time to reply after a question.

- Interpret what children mean rather than accept what they say when it does not make sense.

- Explain jokes, metaphors and sarcasm, as these are not automatically understood.

- Teach idiomatic expressions and appropriate language and behaviour for different situations.

Classroom organisation

- Reduce passive listening to information, and make lessons active participation.
- Provide a quiet, orderly, working environment.
- Make rules, routines and responsibilities clear, and constantly review and display them for regular reference.
- Provide reminders supported by tasks lists and pictures, diagrams or symbols.
- Keep to class routines and explain changes in advance, explaining how they will affect pupils so they know explicitly how they need to respond.
- Encourage visualising so that pupils can learn to create moving pictures in their mind of what is being said.
- Provide opportunities to learn how to communicate in social situations such as the COGS.
- Make sure the child has individual talk time with an adult (e.g. TA, learning mentor or counsellor) so he can be specifically coached in how to perform better.
- Be aware that misunderstandings lead to behaviour/social problems.
- Liaise with parents and other professionals so that there is consistent management of problem.

Spoken communication difficulties will lead to reading and writing problems and are associated with impairments such as dyslexia, dyspraxia and cerebral palsy. They are also very much a part of social and emotional problems that may seem to be the major difficulty in class but are actually secondary to specific problems in using formal language. Details of these are available for reference in Appendix 5.1 for those who are interested.

Habit defects

These defects of articulation or production are due to a wrong position of the lips, tongue, teeth, soft palate and jaws in speaking. No physical problems prevent making correct sounds, but faulty habits are due to lack of correction, resulting in wrong muscular actions. Most bad habits can be corrected by educators, provided:

- they understand what the child is doing wrong with the speech articulators and what should be done to correct the situation
- there is time to spend on a particular child.

The first problem can be helped with the following information, but the second issue is a matter of teaching policy. Perhaps the best conditions are those found in some other countries where short, regular periods are set aside for pupils' individual problems. However, a great deal can be done by general class work, from which everyone can benefit by becoming more aware of the importance of clear speaking.

Principles for speech intervention

Speaking ability is closely linked to hearing, so listening activities should be part of the plan to improve sound recognition. Regularly, have the class monitor the sounds they hear around them; give them contrast pairs, such as *peas/peach* or *pink/wink*, and have them tell you whether they are the same or different.

In most cases, the correcting process has the following stages:

1. Use exercises to strengthen tongue, lips, jaw and soft palate.
2. Have children listen to and make the correct sound as if it were new and independent of words and meaning, so that association does not cause reversion to old habits. Get the child to feel the sound and understand what the speech articulators are doing in making it. A mirror provides helpful feedback.
3. Introduce words containing the sound and use them in speech rhymes orally before seeing the print.
4. Transfer the new pattern to connected speech.

Common speech problems

Lisp (sigmatism)

This is often a substitution of **th** (as in *thin*) for the **s** (as in *sing*). Sometimes, the lisp is due to dropping the sides of the tongue, so that air is channelled out laterally rather than by the middle (lateral sigmatism). We need to strengthen the tongue first. Ask children to pop their little finger into the mouth and roll the sides of the tongue around to hold it fast. Monitor those who find this difficult and mark them for extra practice! Then, draw the tongue tip back from its position between the teeth. This can be done in several ways. Close teeth and try to say **th**, or place a finger between the teeth. Sometimes, it is easier to start with saying **t**, slowing it down and making it slack so it sounds like **ts**. Experiment to find the best way to make a good **s** sound. When established accurately, use it in words – *sing, seat, soap, miss, loss, mass,* etc. Sometimes, a lisp takes the form of **sh** for **s**, and spreading and tensing the lips will often correct this. If not, try from **t** or **ts** as above.

A trickier problem is the **l** for **s** with the sound escaping laterally rather than centrally. Correct from **ts**, but if the habit of tongue raising is too strong, it may be necessary to press the tongue tip firmly against the lower teeth. This makes a reasonable sound to be improved later.

Another error is the use of **f** for **th** (*fing* for *thing*). This follows from uncorrected baby talk, or it may be dialectal. It is a common feature of Midland speech. Concentrate on the tongue position, the tip just showing between the front teeth. This may be done by putting a finger along the lips and blowing. After the first four stages above, comparative exercises help – **f-th**, **f-th** – as do word lists (*three, free, roof, Ruth*). It may be necessary to correct a **v** substitution in words such as *mother, with* etc. After getting the **th** (as in *thing*) correctly formed, say it on a long breath, changing to a voiced **th** (as in *those*). This means turning on the sound in the larynx halfway through the breath: th → TH → th → TH.

Weak r

This results from a tongue tip, that does not curl back sufficiently. Firstly, general tongue exercises will make the tongue more flexible. After this, try from alternatives:

1. With the tongue tip on the upper teeth ridge, curl it slowly back along the roof of the mouth, as far as it will go – to where the hard and soft palates join. Hold it there and say a long '**er**' as in *her*. Then flap it forward and down: **er-rah; er-rah** vigorously.
2. Curl back the tongue as before and say **z**. Put a crooked finger under the tongue to help. Start with **tr** or **dr** as in *train* and *drain*. Although *r* is a tongue-tip sound, many use lips to form it and a defective *r* can be improved by concentrating on these. Push lips forward as if to say *oo*. Keep them there and say *red* like this – **oo…..red**.

Nasality

This is generally the result of an inactive soft palate. Instead of being raised for all sounds except the nasals (*m, n, ng*), it sags into a neutral position, and too much nasality passes through the nose. To correct this, use the previous exercises for the soft palate. In addition, exercises for the lower jaw help, because if the teeth are held too close together, the sound is encouraged to come out through the nose rather than the mouth. Sometimes, inability to use the nose is mistaken for nasality due to blockage from enlarged adenoids or catarrh. Medical advice is required, but breathing and humming exercises assist.

Mumble jumble, slurring, mispronunciation!

These phenomena occur as the result of poor articulation. Exercises are needed for the vigorous use of lips, tongue, teeth, palate and jaws as described. Draw attention to mispronunciations such as '*anythingk*', which is common. Practise the correct word, intoning the final **ng** and play as a game, getting children to think of a word that rhymes, as in *anything, nothing, something,* or *everything* and then putting it in a sentence: *I would like a drink.*

Too loud or too quiet speech

Children start shouting because they are told to speak up. They have not developed projection techniques to throw their voices over distance and so turn up the volume instead! Teach the resonance and projection exercises already described. Inaudible speech may be due to nervousness or uncertainty, so reassure the child and build confidence by praise for behaviour that is moving toward requirements.

Toneless, flat voices

Children have a fantastic voice range, as demonstrated in the playground! However, in class, there are a few with flat, dull voices that do not hold listener interest. Sometimes this reflects boredom and uninterest, so involve pupils in something that grips the imagination. Humorous rhymes and encouragement to talk about something that interests them usually do the trick along with exercises to increase voice range. Boys particularly like counting, starting on the lowest note that can be voiced and going up a tone with each number. It is a challenge to get as high as you can and then reverse the run backward. Children need reminding not to force the tone, so keep attention on easy, natural sound.

English as a second language (ESL)

Many educators experience children arriving in school with little English, whose mother tongue may be Turkish, Chinese, Punjabi, Hindi, Italian and so on. If the language of instruction and social contact is different, educators have a demanding job and are supported by local authority teams. Schools respect the cultural traditions associated with ethnic minority groups so that children feel valued and do not lose their distinctive features. The contrasting lifestyles, social customs, folklore, religions and artistic heritage of different cultural minority groups enrich classroom experience for all children. Nevertheless, those speaking English as a second language have particular problems in learning that language, and they need careful management.

Management

In some areas, children are taught initially in mother tongues, while others withdraw them for English lessons in separate classes. There is a varied response to such practices, some educators feeling that they isolate children. Using the child's mother tongue as a medium of instruction and fostering fluency in the home language are positive but may not be practical or possible.

These issues, however, are contentious and have no straightforward solutions. The majority of the world's children are brought up in multilingual settings. There is little evidence that they will be confused, slower or limited by having to learn more than one language at once. Children naturally learn whatever languages are used around them and are motivated to do so at this stage of their lives.

High-status languages predominate in schools, as those who use them are regarded highly. It is a paradox that we praise a British child who manages enough French to converse on holiday, but fail to acknowledge the achievements of immigrant children that may speak three or four low-regarded languages.

Nevertheless, experts suggest that it takes at least five years for a balanced bilingual ability to emerge (Cummins, 2003). Problems occur for children who grow up with a superficial command of a new language, as they may fail to grasp complex concepts.

If schools had a policy for teaching communication, the problems of ESL children would be considerably eased, as they need direct teaching to become aware of the issues in using English. They have done brilliantly on the COGS because it has made them aware of what they need to concentrate on to become competent English speakers. Pronunciation is a particular issue, as some English sounds may not be in the repertoire of a first language. Teaching objectives should include the following:

- Emphasise eye contact – this needs explaining, as adult eye contact would appear rude in Indian cultures.
- Provide a secure, accepting environment with familiar routines.
- Accompany your own activity with talk.
- Restrict the number in contact with a child and introduce them to other children with another adult present initially.
- Separate the child confidently from parents; smile and be upbeat.
- Arrange play with one adult or child and encourage turn taking.
- During stories or explanation, involve the child in non-verbal activities to motivate attention.
- Encourage participation in group rhymes, songs and jingles.
- Locate and refer to everyday objects, people and activities by name.
- Indicate needs through gestures and words.
- Initiate interaction with a request for things.
- Make sure the child has vocabulary for familiar items and events.
- Use pictures/objects to make associations.

Review

All the suggestions for helping impaired communication are comparatively easy but need commitment from interested adults who understand the value of pleasant and effective communication (Pertemps Survey, 2004; Sage et al., 2004). Children with problems benefit from more direct help with speaking, but some are repelled by exercises. It is a challenge, however, to make them fun and engaging. They are beneficial in sharpening awareness of voice dynamics, which conveys meaning, so improving comprehension as well as helping children change their speaking to more normal patterns. Support is particularly important for those who have specific physical, emotional or habit problems. They are likely to become speech conscious and be ridiculed unless helped to overcome difficulties. Hearing and visual problems appear more common in classrooms, and excessive stress is a reason for this. The attempt to make children read before their nervous systems are ready to deal with two-dimensional form is a factor here.

   In conclusion, attention to all facets of the communication process, and not just speaking and listening components, has dramatic personal and academic benefits, as is well documented in research summarised by Brigman et al (1999). We all want better behaved and more motivated pupils, and we will have them if communication takes pride of place in the curriculum. So, good talking and good luck!

Key Points

- Many children suffer from physical, emotional or habit problems that interfere with communication.
- Understanding the issues regarding communication difficulties is the key to managing them successfully.
- Problems are within not only the children but also the class, so that adjustments are needed to reduce these.
- Although it is difficult to monitor each child's speaking performance, regular talk opportunities in class will not only help children to practise but also give them a chance to be coached by adults.
- Speech problems are the biggest hindrance to personal and academic success, and it is worth becoming expert in their management.

Appendices

The Appendices are listed by chapter and contain additional information, tables and exercises to support the text.

Appendix 1.1

Are you an effective communicator?

Try this checklist and reflect on your strengths and areas for development

Establishing relationships

- Do you express your feelings easily and clearly?
- Do you allow pupils and colleagues to know what sort of person you are?
- Do you let pupils know you respect them?
- Do you give pupils routine, roles and responsibilities in the contexts in which you work?

Presenting a positive example

- Do you come over as cheerful and confident?
- Do you treat pupils fairly and firmly, and reward rather than punish?
- Do you use positive rather than negative commands?
- Do you make expectations clear, and praise when these are met?

Supporting learning

- Do you develop pupil's self-esteem and confidence?
- Do you differentiate tasks to suit needs?
- Do you help pupils to set goals and plan to meet these?
- Do you vary communication to suit the audience?

Listening

- Do you listen without becoming distracted?
- Do you visualise what you are hearing so that you remember?

- Do you record key ideas?
- Do you summarise what you have heard?

Verbal behaviour

- Do you address others in a polite, friendly way?
- Do you adjust questions to suit a pupil's thinking and understanding-level?
- Do you give clear instructions and explanations?
- Do you use words and sentences that others understand?

Non-verbal behaviour

- Do you maintain eye contact with those you talk to?
- Do you use an expressive voice to help others attend to what you say?
- Do you normally smile, look relaxed and appear pleasant?
- Do you use facial expressions and gestures to support your words?

What is your view of yourself as a communicator?

Tips for dealing with difficult behaviour – example: Mark

1. **Use *I* statements**: *Mark, **I** need you to listen* – is more effective than *Mark, **you** aren't listening.*
2. **Repeat statement if ignored** in same voice tone and volume to show firmness.
3. **Say how you feel**: *Mark, I feel cross when you talk as I can't listen to Mrs Brown* – focus on you, not pupil.
4. **Check understanding**: *Mark, you said you didn't understand, is that right?* – clarifies.
5. **Interpret cause**: *Mark, you're not happy with me but not saying so* – establishes truth.
6. **Give positive feedback first**: *Mark, thanks for listening. Now, I need you to finish this by break.*
7. **Compromise**: *Mark, you didn't understand the lesson. Come and see me at 12.30 for help.*
8. **Control feelings**: If angry, count to 10 before speaking.
9. **Resolve conflict**: *You're upset about this work. I need it to be done. Let's solve this together.*
10. **Make goal clear**: Clarify behaviour; state effect; refer to incident; allow space for response:
    Mark, chatting in class annoys me. It means I can't hear Mrs Brown talking. Can you listen silently so I can get the information to help you?

Appendix 2.1

Ages and stages of brain growth

Conception to 15 months: cerebellum development

- survival systems: breathing, sleeping, waking, eating, elimination
- sensory development: balance, hearing, touch, smell and seeing
- motor development: reflexes integrate into neck, arm and leg movement.

15 months to 4.5 years: limbic system development

- emotional exploration: feelings, emotions and expression
- social development: memory and relationships – self and others
- large movement proficiency: walking, running, jumping, climbing.

4.5–7 years: global hemisphere development (usually right brain)

- sees whole picture: top-down processing: deduces the gist
- builds images from movement and feeling: rhythm, emotion, intuition
- talks to develop thoughts: outer speech.

7–9 years: linear hemisphere development (usually left brain)

- processes detail: bottom-up processing: induces from details
- develops complex language (clauses): understands sounds, letters, words in writing
- uses logic/linear processing to solve problems; develops techniques.

8–9 years: frontal lobe development

- fine motor proficiency: manual dexterity for writing and two-dimensional eye focus (fovea)
- internal language formed to regulate tasks and behaviour (inner language).

9–12 years: increased right and left brain connections through corpus callosum

- right and left brain integration
- proficient top-down and bottom-up processing.

12–16 years: hormonal changes of puberty

- body conscious: preoccupied with body functions of self and others
- increases social and community interactions.

16–21 years: thinking skills extend

- plans for future: considers ideas and possibilities
- emotional and social maturity: independence and coping skills.

20–30 years: frontal lobes refine

- formal reasoning: high level of thinking, reflection and insight
- emotional refinement: altruism, love, understanding and compassion
- fine motor skills: develops and sustains intricate manual activities.

30 years onward: refinements of physical and mental abilities

- hands and face: greater finger and face agility for improved expression
- experience brings perspective, understanding, acceptance and wisdom.

Appendix 4.1

Articulation agility

We speak at the rate of around 180 words a minute in ordinary conversation. Does this surprise you? It represents a great deal of movement and around 400 sounds, ringing the changes on the 45 different vowels and consonants that make up our language. All these intricate, delicate adjustments take place within the small, mouth cavity. The ability to manipulate these presents a feat comparable to that of a pianist who rapidly and dexterously changes finger positions to make an infinite number of variations. The speaker, therefore, needs help with each of the speech organs, especially the hard-working tongue and lips, in order to produce a fluent performance.

Vigour

Vigorous speech comes from breath force and strength of articulation. We aim for energetic speech that is not too loud. Four speech organs are involved – the lower jaw, tongue, lips and soft palate (uvula). The jaw has already been tackled in regard to resonance, but the other three are catered for in the following exercises.

Tongue

1. Exercises for the front of the tongue: think of it as a pendulum – move it slowly and strongly from side to side outside your mouth; pretend to lick ice cream, first normally and then from the bottom of the cone; flatten the tongue like a pancake and bunch it like a banana.
2. Sounds and noises: try the train running smoothly – *tiddly pom—tiddly pom* and then getter faster – *tiddlypom, tiddlypom*; the propeller spinning – *rrrrrrrrrr*; the drum – *drrrr, drrrr, drrrr*; the horse ambling *t-t-t-t-t-t-t* and then trotting *tttt-tttt-tttt-tttt*.
3. Practise tongue-tip action: *la-la-la-la, ta-ta-ta-ta, ra-ra-ra-ra* (tongue tip curled back).

4. Pretend your tongue is a door knocker: *t –t – t*, and try this poem:

Rat–a–tat–tat, rat—a—tat–tat,

It's Postman Pat in his very black hat.

Every morning at half-past eight,

You hear the bang at our garden gate,

Then the thud of the mail on the polished floor.

But before I blink, Pat's away from the door,

And he's up the path of the very next house.

Watch out, postman, there's Minnie the mouse!

Lips

1. Exercise lips by making window shapes: porthole – *round*; church window – *tall and narrow*; car window – *long and wide*; house – *as square as you can*!
2. Shape lips as if you were a goldfish, crocodile or cod..
3. Make these sounds and noises: lorry revving up: *vvvvv-vvvvv-vvvvv*; motor boat starting up: *pt-pt-pt-pt-pt*; cars waiting to go: *brrr-brrr-brrr-brrr*; pony puffing in the field: *pwwww* (blow through vibrating lips).
4. Imitate sounds: water dripping slowly – *p---p---p---p*; pouring liquid from a bottle and speed increasing – *p-p-p-p-p-ppppppppppppp*; motor boat working slowly, and then repeat speeding up the engine – *p-------p--------p------p—p—p—p—p-p-p-p-*

Try this rhyme with two groups – one for each line.

1. Biff!, bang!, biff!, bang!, bash!
2. Who's that making a crash?
3. Biff!, bang!, biff!, bang!, bash!
4. It's Dustman Dan, on his weekly dash!

Soft palate

Try these following exercises to get the soft palate (uvula) moving. This hangs down from the end of the hard palate (the roof of the mouth). It needs to be agile to lift quickly and cut off nasal passages so that air passes cleanly through the mouth for articulation of all sounds except *m, n, ng*. Round lips tightly and draw breath in.

1. Say the word *ping-* sustaining the *ng* sound and then cut it off with *K, ping-k*. Repeat with *wing-k*; *link-k*; *ring-k*; *sing-k*; *ding-k*.
2. Try sound babbles: *pm,pm,pm,pm*; *k-ng,k-ng,k-ng,k-ng*.

General exercises

Action words. Think of words to describe energetic movements: *push, pull, heave, haul, kick, roll, jump, throw, hit, hurl, lob, slap, punch, twist, twirl, hop, skip, run.*

Noise words. Think of words that suggest strong sounds, and say them with energy rather than volume: *bang, crash, thump, bump, crack, pop, hiss, shout, sing, slash, saw, swish, slosh, strum, flip, shake, shudder, drill, tap, hammer, rev, hit.*

Since vigour is physical, any bodily activity can help speech as long as there is some link. In cricket, you hit the ball hard to get your runs, so give a similar whack to words. Look elsewhere in this appendix for further ideas to develop agile speech.

Exercises that can also help to build sound and sentence patterns

Tongue-twisters are a wonderful way to achieve agility, and are good fun. They twist the tongue, lips and brain, so they are good all-rounders! They call for the art that conceals art, as none is spoken successfully if it sounds difficult. Repeat each three times, keeping the thought clear as well as the speech:

- red leather, yellow leather
- what a lot of little, light bottles
- Betty Brown's best British butter
- deep freeze peas, please
- thin the three thick thistles
- Peter Perkins's precious, plump pears.

Some tongue-twisters lend themselves to speaking by two or three voices:

1. Is it a thin fish or a thick fish?
2. It's a thin fish with a thick fin.

1. Once there was a selfish shellfish slumbering on the salty seashore.
2. Why was the salty, seashore shellfish selfish?
3. Because the selfish shellfish slumbered on the salty seashore by himself.

Language use

Effective use of language depends on the following aspects:

vocabulary: general and specialist words, which transmit spoken and written words

grammar: parts of speech used in sentences

syntax: conventions that govern sentence formation

style: words, sentence structure and tone adopted for a specific communication purpose

inference:	interpretation of nuances and shades of meaning in, between and behind words
judgement:	critical evaluation of what is said/read to reflect on its effect and modify if necessary
awareness:	rapport with the recipient so the message can be received and understood
spelling:	reproduction of words in their accepted written form
punctuation:	writing marks that help the meaning and convey the feelings of the writer.

Useful definitions

Sentence:	a group of words that conveys a complete meaning. It must have a subject plus finite verb, begin with a capital letter and end with a full stop in written form.
Simple sentence:	a sentence with a single subject plus finite verb in its predicate.
Complex sentence:	a sentence with two or more main or dependent clauses.
Phrase:	a group of words which are related in sense and are often introduced by a <u>preposition</u>: *on his way to work, at the moment, in the top drawer* or <u>conjunction</u>: *after a busy day at work, as soon as possible.* Phrases do not contain finite verbs but can be introduced with participles: '*Opening the door*, Luke saw a black cat sitting on the window ledge'.
Clause:	a group of words forming part of a sentence and possessing a subject and finite verb. Clauses are linked by conjunctions: *He arrived late* <u>because</u> *the train was delayed*.
Main clause:	joining main clauses with coordinating conjunctions may make complex sentences: *She paused* and *she had a sandwich*; <u>then</u> *she resumed work*
Dependent clause:	This clause cannot stand alone and is linked to a main one by a subordinating conjunction: <u>As</u> *the weather is bad, we shall come by car*, <u>even though</u> *it means delaying the repair to the cracked windscreen*.

Grammar

Words are the building blocks of a sentence and carry out specific functions.

nouns	naming words, which act as labels for things – objects, people, places, events, ideas, etc. Nouns naming real, physical things, such as *cup* and *spoon*, are *concrete nouns*. Those, that express thoughts, ideas, and feelings, such as *effect* and *communication*, are called *abstract nouns*. There are other sub-divisions:

- common: everyday objects or ideas – *pen, weight, library*
- proper: names for people, places, art works – *Rosemary, England, Mona Lisa* (capital letters)
- collective: names for groupings or collections – *class, team, bench* (of magistrates).

Pronouns Identifying words that replace nouns:

- people: *I, you, him, her, mine, ours*
- things: *it, that*.

- Question forms: *<u>Who</u> is going? <u>What</u> do you think?*
- Completion forms: *I hurt <u>myself</u>.*
- Further information forms: *The girl <u>who</u> is blond. The book, <u>which</u> is about language.*

Articles These define nouns: *the* class, *a* lesson, *an* idea.

Adjectives These words describe and extend the meaning of nouns and pronouns, usually coming before them but occasionally after. *The <u>exhausted</u> teacher promptly dismissed <u>her</u> class because she was <u>busy</u>.*

Adjectives may denote possession (*<u>my</u> house*), identify something (*<u>These</u> ideas*) or introduce a question (*<u>What</u> time is it?*).

Verbs These convey actions, identify thought processes or denotes-tates of being:

- *He <u>cooked</u> a meal and <u>ate</u> it.*
- *She <u>considered</u> the proposal carefully.*
- *The teacher <u>was</u> aware of the difficulty.*

Verbs are used actively to express the actions of the doer: *He <u>read</u> the report.*

They are used *passively* to make the doer the agent of the action: *The report was <u>read</u> by him.*

Passive verbs make the message more distant and impersonal.

Adverbs These extend the meaning of verbs or adjectives: *He spoke <u>slowly</u> and <u>clearly</u>. We need an <u>extremely</u> fast typist.* Most adverbs are recognised by their *-ly* endings. They indicate *how, when, where, to what extent, how many*, etc.

Conjunctions These are linking words to join ideas together and may begin a sentence:

<u>As</u> it's hot, you may go now. Buy fish <u>and</u> chips. The book is short <u>but</u> contains everything.

Conjunctions (*and, but, next, then, yet*) may link ideas that could stand alone. *The book is short. It contains everything.*

Conjunctions can link a main and dependent idea: *They bought a car <u>although</u> it was costly.*

Commonly used conjunctions are *when, where, why, what, as, since, because, although, though, even though, if, whether, so that, in order that, with the result that, after, unless, as soon as.*

Paired sets of conjunctions are *either/or, neither/nor, both/and, not only/but also.*

Prepositions These are locating words coming in front of nouns or pronouns:

The box is <u>under</u> the bed. They may form parts of verbs: I must get <u>down</u> to finishing this book.

Interjections These are words expressing feelings or emotions used frequently in direct speech. *'Whew!' That was a close shave* (relief). *Oh! What a beautiful dress!* (delight).

Syntax

Syntax is the patterns in which *sentences* are constructed.

What is a sentence? It is a group of words which conveys a complete meaning with *subject* (noun or noun group) and *predicate* (finite verb or finite verb plus enlargers or object).

Subject	**Predicate**
I like	*chocolate.*
The tired, old lady	*went straight to bed.*
The last, weekday train	*is at 11.30 p.m.*

What is a subject? Subjects are *common* or *proper* nouns, which are the *doer* words or word groups governing the actions of finite verbs: *<u>The report</u> is finished. <u>Joan</u> is away today.* They may be *pronouns* (*<u>They</u> are gorgeous!*) and take the form of a *phrase* (*<u>Rushing a three-course lunch</u> gave him an awful stomach-ache*) or a *clause* (*That <u>you were ignorant of the rules</u> makes no difference*). The terms *phrase* and *clause* are explained in the definitions at the end of this section. Although subjects usually precede verbs, additional ideas about them can be inserted between (*My student, a hard working member of the class, will do well in the examinations*).

What is a predicate? This may include not just the finite verb but also words that enlarge the meaning (*I washed thoroughly*) or provide additional information (*I washed with hot water*).

Some need an *object* (action receiver) to complete the meaning (*I washed my jeans*). Therefore, simple sentences may be constructed as follows:

- subject plus finite verb
- subject plus finite verb plus enlargers
- subject plus finite verb plus object.

What is a finite verb? All sentences require finite verbs, carrying out the *action* of the *doer* or *subject word*. They must meet three requirements as in: *I washed*. (singular, third person, past tense).

- *a number*: singular or plural
- *a person*: first, second or third
- *a tense*: past, present, future or conditional.

When sentences contain a single subject and a single finite verb (*I washed*), they are called *simple*. When more than one subject and finite verb are used in linked groups, they are called *complex* (*I and my friend Sue washed our jeans before we went to the disco*).

Appendix Table 4.1

Verb tenses: Infinitive: *to write*   Present participle: *writing*   Past participle: *written*

Tenses	Active (he)	Passive (the book)
Present		
simple	writes	is written
continuous	is writing	is being written
Past		
simple	wrote	was written
continuous	was writing	was being written
Perfect		
simple	has written	has been written
continuous	has been writing	
Past perfect		
simple	had written	had been written
continuous	had been writing	
Future		
simple	will write	will be written
continuous	will be writing	
Future perfect		
simple	will have written	will have been written
continuous	will have been writing	
Conditional		
simple	would have written	would have been written
continuous	would have been writing	

How are verbs used?

Finite verbs are governed by subjects and possess number, person and tense. When verbs literally convey ideas of action, they are easily identifiable: *The teacher cut the paper. Jack painted his picture carefully*.

Many verbs, however, express *abstract* notions: *He loves his bed in the mornings*.

Some verbs consist of more than one word: *I shall have left for work before the post comes*.

A knowledge of tenses is necessary to recognise verbs successfully as well as to understand their *active* and *passive* use.

Active and passive

Verbs which take objects, when used actively, convey the action of the subject or doer to an action receiver or object: *Rosie* (subject) *typed* (finite verb) *the chapter of the book* (object).

The same idea, however, may be expressed in a passive form. Here the object becomes the grammatical subject of the sentence, and the active subject becomes an agent of the passive. *The report* (subject) *was typed* (finite verb) *by Rosie* (agent).

The verb *to be* and sometimes also the verb *to have* are used with the past participle of the verb to form the passive structures of verbs: *Is being typed, was typed, has been typed*.

Verb forms as adjectives and nouns

There are two parts of the verb that are used in sentences, not as verbs, but as nouns or adjectives:

Present participle as adjective: *The pouring rain drenched my clothes*.

Past participle as adjective: *The typed book is ready for the publisher*.

Present participle as noun: *Her going was very sudden*.

What is an object?

Objects in sentences receive the action of the verb. Some verbs, which need objects to complete the sense, are called *transitive*. Verbs, which do not need an object to convey the meaning, are called *intransitive*. It is helpful to think of objects as answering the question *What? Mary* (subject) *made* (finite verb) *a cake* (object). What did Mary make?

Some objects take the form of word groups: *Pat wrote a long and interesting report*. Others take the form of clauses: *Ted hit what appeared to be a sliced shot of the ball*. When transitive verbs are used in the passive form, the object of the active voice of the verb becomes the subject: _A long and interesting report was written_ by Pat. _What appeared to be a sliced shot of the ball_ was hit by Ted.

Enlarging intransitive verbs

When verbs are used intransitively (not needing an object), adverbial words or expressions may be used to extend meaning: _The meal went on for quite a while_.

What are complex sentences?

Many sentences are composed of two or more clauses with the following relationships:

Main clause plus main clause: _She played tennis and she did not finish the game until dusk_.

Main clause plus dependent clause: _She wanted to go early because she had a bad headache_.

Main and dependent clauses can be combined in a number of ways:

- dependent: _although it wasn't convenient,_
- main: _she played tennis until dusk_
- dependent   _because she wanted to finish the game._

Ideas are linked in this way to provide variety and show the relationship between ideas. All clauses must have a subject and finite verb. Dependent ones cannot stand alone and need to be accompanied by a main clause. It is easy to lose control in complex sentences: _The new teacher, who wanted to make a good impression on the first day in her new class, although she was feeling nervous because the place was unfamiliar, despite the friendly smiles of the pupils._ Here, we wait in vain for the main verb to follow _The new teacher_. To avoid this problem, it is wise to shorten the structure and create two sentences: _The new teacher wanted to make a good impression on the first day in her new class. She received friendly smiles from the pupils but was feeling nervous because the place was unfamiliar._

Appendix Table 4.2 English consonants: voiced/voiceless

	1	2	3	4	5	6	7	8	9
A									
plosive	p, **b**			t, **d**				k, **g**	
affricate					**tr, dr**	ch, **dg**			
fricative		f, **v**	th, **th**	s, **z**		sh, **su**			h
B									
nasal	**m**			**n**				**ing**	
frictionless									
continuant	**w**				**r**		**j**		

Consonants are <u>normally paired</u>: *voiceless* (no sound) and *voiced* (sound). Voiced are marked with bold face.

1. bilabial (made with lips together – p, **b**, **m**, **w**)
2. labio-dental (made with top teeth biting bottom lip – f ,**v**)
3. dental (made with tongue tip between teeth – th as in *teeth*; **th** as in *mother*)
4. alveolar (tongue tip on ridge behind top teeth – t, **d**, s, **z**, **n**, **l**)
5. post-alveolar (tongue tip on ridge behind top teeth and released – tr, **dr**, **r**)
6. palato-alveolar (tongue tip on ridge behind top teeth and moving to the palate – ch, **dg**, sh, **su**)
7. palatal (tongue towards the palate – **j**)
8. velar (made with the back of the tongue – k, **g**, **ing**)
9. glottal (air expelled strongly when the glottis is open – h)

A – total closure or stricture of the air stream
plosive – air stopped completely – p, **b**, t, **d**, k, **g**
affricate – air stop with slow release – t**r**, **dr**
fricative – air stream modified by lip/tongue/glottal movements – f, **v**, th, **th**, s, **z**, sh, **su**, h

B – partial closure or unimpeded oral or nasal escape
nasal – air release through nose and not mouth – **m**, **n**, **ing**
lateral – air released from the side of the tongue – **l**
frictionless continuant – continuing sounds similar to vowels – **w**, **r**, **l**

Appendix Table 4.3 Vowels made in the front, centre or back of the mouth

Mouth position	Front	Central	Back
Closed	h<u>ee</u>d		h<u>oo</u>t
	h<u>i</u>d		h<u>oo</u>d
Half-closed			
	h<u>ea</u>d	h<u>ea</u>rd	h<u>oa</u>rd
Half-open	h<u>a</u>d		h<u>o</u>d
Open		h<u>u</u>t	h<u>a</u>rd

These are the common vowels in standard formation.

Appendix 5.1

Dyslexia

Dyslexia in literal translation means *difficulty with words,* and it is the inability to reach expected standards in reading, writing and spelling. It is a complex neurological condition affecting up to 10% of people, especially males.

Characteristics

- slow information-processing for spoken and written language
- limited short-term memory
- sequencing and organisational difficulties
- tiredness
- uneven performance
- frustration possibly leading to bad behaviour.

Reading is slow, with problems in gaining meaning from content. People with dyslexia describe print as swirling and have tracking difficulties, frequently losing their place. They experience difficulties in blending and segmenting sounds in words due to inadequate phonological processing. They make constant errors with high-frequency words (*and, the, but*) but may cope better with difficult words that are more easily visualised.

Writing is normally of an inadequate standard, displaying letter confusions and distortions (*tired* for *tried,* etc.). Spelling is often bizarre and work messy.

Management

People with dyslexia are often good lateral thinkers and do well in right-brain activities such as art, drama and sport. They benefit from an oral-to-literate approach, developing and organising ideas first through talk, before recording them. Similarly, with reading, they are helped by talking about the story and gaining an overview of the meaning before decoding the words. Getting them into reading through action rhymes is successful. They learn to integrate sound and movement, and then map on the written word to a sequence they have established. It is essential to develop their visualisation (Sage, 2003).

Tips

- Work from strong skills.
- Use a judicial multisensory approach as outlined above.
- Use pictures, flow charts and plans, and, using visualisation strategies, talk about ideas before reading or writing about them.
- Use audiotapes to record information before writing it.
- ICT and voice-recognition software is helpful.
- Employ coloured overlays, line trackers and book marks if this helps.
- Allow time for tasks and give constant praise for efforts.
- Keep a wordbook for writing in subject lessons and learn these in a Look, Copy, Cover and Recall strategy. This is more successful than a structured spelling programme, as the words are needed and used constantly, providing repetition and motivation to learn. A thesaurus from age 8 is a boon.

Classroom organisation

- Provide a mind map of the lesson on wall display.
- Teach study skills that are vital for children with dyslexia but helpful to all.
- Reduce board work and never ask the child with dyslexia to copy from this.
- Make sure tests are short and frequent rather than long and occasional.
- Provide help for tests/exams and arrange for extra time.
- Allow work to be done on a computer (laptops are a must).
- Provide oral as well as written tests, as children with dyslexia do better on these.
- Provide extra help such as the COGS, which allows children to develop thinking, processing and expressing skills in both speech and writing.

Movement problems: dyspraxia and cerebral palsy (CP)

Dyspraxia is a motor impairment in which people are unable to perform purposive movements, although they are not paralysed or deficient in muscle coordination. The cause is immaturity in processing information so that messages are not transmitted properly. There may be problems in coordinating fine and gross movements, perception and thought. About 5% of the population are affected, and four times as many boys as girls are reported. They present as clumsy and disorganised, often with communication impairment and dyslexia.

Characteristics: problems with

- crawling, walking and talking
- understanding spatial language: *in/on/in front/behind, etc.*
- following instructions
- concentration
- laterality

- picking up small objects and holding pencils, pens and paintbrushes
- jigsaws and sorting activities
- dressing and eating
- games, movement and music
- recognising dangerous situations
- social skills
- posture and body awareness
- tiredness and irritability.

Management

Educators need advice on how to facilitate good posture and movement, perception, speech accuracy and fluency. Here are things to remember:

- provide extra supervision and give encouragement to stay on task
- make instructions short and simple, checking for understanding (note that children with dyspraxia do not understand sarcasm or irony)
- limit handwriting and use a laptop to record, as writing is laborious
- break tasks into small steps
- use colour and chunking to aid in following text
- teach strategies to remember and facilitate self-organisation
- understand that growth spurts accentuate basic movement problems.

Classroom organisation

- Position pupil with a direct view of the teacher and minimal distractions.
- Make sure seating allows both feet on the floor for postural stability and provide a sloping surface at elbow height for work.
- Limit board work and copying, as it is impossible to look, remember and write.
- Be aware of limitations in movement activities and give roles that allow success.
- Provide a buddy to help with tricky situations.
- Secure paper with Blu-Tack for writing or drawing.
- Keep in touch with parents and other professionals for advice.

Dealing with physical causes of speech difficulty is usually a long-term process, demanding patience and praise. Imagine the agony of speaking when there is something physically stopping you. Try talking with pebbles in the mouth and you will see what I mean!

Cerebral palsy (CP)

This term defines non-progressive brain disorders of posture and movement. The damage happens before or after birth (as in infections or strangulation by the umbilical cord). Difficulties with vision, hearing, thinking and speaking are common, and about one in three of such children is epileptic. Severely affected children are educated in special schools/units, but children with milder forms are in mainstream education, appearing as poorly coordinated and clumsy.

Speech is affected because of the difficulty in making precise movements accurately; this is known as dysarthria.

Types and characteristics (forms often coexist)

Spastic (75% of CP population) means *stiff,* and sufferers have stiffened muscles and decreased joint movements due to cerebral cortex damage. There are three types:

- hemiplegia – one side of the body affected
- diplegia – legs affected more than arms
- quadraplegia – arms and legs affected.

Athetoid defines a rapid change from floppy to tense muscles, resulting in writhing and involuntary movements as a result of damage to the basal ganglia.

Ataxic refers to difficult balance and poor spatial awareness caused by cerebellum damage. Sufferers walk unsteadily with shaky, jerky movements. This is a rare form.

Management

Although there is no cure, posture and muscle control are improved by physiotherapy, perception and spatial awareness by occupational therapy, and communication by speech and language therapy. Those with severe forms of movement disturbance need computerised aids to communicate. Adults must position children correctly to function effectively, and close cooperation with therapists is essential. Many regarded as clumsy are at the low end of the CP continuum, and although they might not have found their way to medical specialists, they will benefit from help to improve balance, posture and movement coordination.

Tips

- Remember that the physically impaired child may be above average in intelligence.
- Promote understanding of the pupil's needs through subjects such as physical, social and health education (PSHE).
- Communicate with parents and experts for correct handling.
- Coordinate therapy – it is important to be aware of breathing, feeding, posture and movement techniques.
- Pair the pupil with a suitable buddy, but do not overburden them.
- Use ICT – Inclusive Technology and Semerc – especially for communication.
- Use audio-visual aids as support.

Classroom organisation

- Assess physical access – ramps, toilets and classroom layout.
- TAs need to be trained in the use of aids such as head pointers, individualised wheelchairs, electronic devices and adaptive equipment.

- Be clear about associated difficulties such as visual perception, hearing, vision and speaking.
- Ensure a good position for pupils to view class activities because they will not be able to adjust themselves to hear and see like others.
- Work on the class's understanding of differences and their accommodation.

Social, emotional and behavioural difficulties (SEBD)

Emotional and behavioural difficulties disrupt others and cause social and educational problems. There are various causes, such as abuse, neglect, physical and mental illness, sensory/physical impairment and psychological trauma. SEBD refers to a range of difficulties, including neurosis, antisocial behaviour and psychosis. According to the Office for National Statistics, 10% of children have a mental health disorder. The national children's mental health charity *Young Minds* believes that up to 40% of youngsters in cities have emotional and behaviour problems. There is considerable literature to suggest that these impairments are often secondary to those of limited formal communication ability.

Types and characteristics

Neurosis

- anxiety disorder (symptoms: sleeping problems, aches and pains)
- phobia (irrational fear – dog phobia is common in children)
- obsessive/compulsive behaviour (ritualistic, pointless routines interfering with living)
- avoidance/withdrawal (clinging, fearful, tearful and solitary)
- hypochondria (worry about health)
- hysteria (regress or lose memory)
- depression (feelings of worthlessness shown in withdrawal)
- eating/sleeping disorders and incontinence.

Antisocial behaviour (conduct disorder)

- disruption (annoying behaviours)
- aggression
- uncooperativeness
- delinquency.

Psychotic behaviour

- schizophrenia (occurs in adolescence and is characterised by thought disorder)
- dementia (reduced intellectual abilities due to damage or deterioration in brain tissue)
- toxic confusion (due to drug abuse or accidental poisoning such as lead)
- reactive psychosis (occurs in times of stress and demonstrated in lack of contact with reality and bizarre behaviour).

Management

SEBD responds to communication training, behaviour modification, psychotherapy, cognitive therapy and counselling. Drugs help depression, and doctors suggest that about 10% of children are now so stressed that they need medical support. The prognosis tends to be poorer for children with antisocial behaviour than for those with neurotic problems. Some children show more than one type of difficulty. Work with families and support in the community are essential. Management is broadly similar to those with communication difficulties.

Glossary

Chapter 1

Clarity: clear thoughts and sound expression.

COGS: Communication Opportunity Group Scheme.

Coherence: ideas assembled in an orderly, logical fashion so that they are meaningful.

Conduct: the manner of communicating and use of feedback.

Content: considering choice of vocabulary, structure and topic focus to suit purpose.

Convention: rules that govern word arrangements and behaviour.

Foundation stage: stage prior to National Curriculum, for children aged under 5 years. In primary schools, this is usually 4+.

Inferential comprehension: 'reading between the lines'; understanding meaning that is implied, not actually stated.

Literal comprehension: take words at face value without reference to context e.g. pull up your socks, teacher–pupil means work harder.

Narrative thinking assembly of ideas and their expression.

Reference: making connection with information already given, as when a pronoun stands for a subject or object (gives fluency and rhythm and avoids repetition).

Value-added: a measure of the quality of input taken from where children were at the beginning of a teaching period (baseline assessment), and where they are at the end of this period.

Chapter 2

Analysis: the ability to see patterns in formation.

Bottom up: a psychological process involving building up meaning from individual components.

Emotional literacy: understanding of feelings; stability.

Ethological theory: this targets inborn, instinctive patterns of interaction.

Expansion: repetition of what has just been said, expanding it into a complete grammatical sentence.

Imitation: copy of a model.

Language acquisition device: suggested by Chomsky, to explain predisposition of humans to developing language.

Phonology: the pronounciation system of a language.

Pragmatics: study of language in context.

Proto-word: first utterance that sounds similar to a word in pitch and tone, but is not phonetically correct, often standing for a real word. The child understands something of the purpose of communication, but not all.

Psychoanalytic approach: analysing behaviour in terms of sexual development.

Register: form of language used in certain circumstances; also means range of tones produced by the voice.

Reinforcement: reiteration of information already given to confirm or help form meaning.

Self-concept: how one sees oneself.

Self-esteem: measure of pride, belief or respect.

Self-image: view of one's own personality and abilities – different from self-concept in that one might manipulate the image for particular purposes.

Semantics: study of word meanings.

Sociolinguistics: study of how language-use varies in different social situations.

Syntax: grammatical structure or ordering of elements in sentences and text.

Top-down: is the psychological process involved in assembling the overall meaning of something.

Chapter 3

Discourse: naturally occurring connected spoken or written discourse.

Plenary: summary of a lesson, or part of it.

Chapter 4

Articulation: place, manner and movement in making speech sounds to indicate meaning.

Dialect: form of language including regional variation of vocabulary and/or grammar.

Emphasis: stress on particular words or parts of words in a sentence.

Forward production: sound produced in mouth rather than throat (background production).

Nasal resonance: applied to sounds such as **ng**, which are made when the soft palate lowers to allow breath to pass through the nose.

Oral resonance: refers to the way breath enters the mouth chamber and carries the sound waves with it.

Phonetics: the science of speech sounds.

Phrasing: using a breath of air to string words together 'like beads' to make sense to the listener.

Pitch: vocal range – high, medium, low tones.

Projection: bringing the voice forward and using it to its full extent (so that people can hear at a distance without the need for the speaker to shout).

Tune: refers to fall and rise of voice to indicate purpose – e.g. statement – falling tune; question – rising tune.

Chapter 5

Conductive loss: hearing loss as a result of difficulty in transmission of sound.

Delay: normal pattern but slow in development.

Deviance: development that does not follow normal lines.

Dyslexia: related to a range of difficulties with coding and decoding text and print.

Dyspraxia: difficulty in organising action/or ideas.

Expressive language: verbal and non-verbal use of language to express meaning.

Idiomatic expression: a distinctive expression whose meaning is not determinable from the meaning of individual words, as in *It's raining cats and dogs*.

Organic: referring to a type of disorder with an explicit medical cause, such as aphasia caused by damage or abnormality in the cerebral cortex.

Prosody: refers to the way intonation and stress are used to provide rhythm and fluency when talking.

Receptive language: understanding the meaning of the actions and speech of other people in relation to context.

Semantic pragmatics: the study of how meaning is achieved through social use of language.

Sensory loss: an impairment of one or more of the input channels of hearing, sight, movement, feeling, taste and smell that would result in a reduction of information-processing capacity.

Visual acuity: a measure of the ratio between the size of print and the distance one needs to be from that print in order to read it effectively; what is measured to test short- or long-sightedness.

References

Ainsworth, M.D.S. (1973) 'The development of infant–mother attachment', in B.M. Caldwell and H.N. Ricciuti, (eds), *Review of Child Development Research* (vol. 3). Chicago: University of Chicago Press.

Alexander, R. (2003) *New Perspectives on Spoken English: Discussion Papers.* London: QCA.

Alexander, R. (2004) *Towards Dialogic Teaching: Rethinking Classroom Talk.* Cambridge: Dialogos.

Bandura, A. (1973) *Aggression, A Social Learning Analysis.* Engelwood Cliffs, NJ: Prentice-Hall.

Bell, N. (1991) *Visualising and Verbalizing,* (rev. edn.) Paso Robles, CA: Academy of Reading Publications.

Bowlby, J. (1969) *Attachment and Loss.* Vol 1: *Attachment.* New York: Basic Books.

Boyer, E.L. (1992) *Read to Learn: A Mandate for the Nation.* Princeton, NJ: Carnegie Foundation for the Advancement of Teaching.

Brigman, G., Lane, D. and Switzer, D. (1999) 'Teaching children school success skills', *Journal of Educational Research*, 92 (6): 323–9.

Browne, N. (2004) *Gender Equity in the Early Years.* Maidenhead: Open University Press.

Bruner, J.S. (1966) *Towards a Theory of Instruction.* New York: Newton.

Bruner, J.S. (1990) *Acts of Meaning.* Cambridge, MA: Havard University Press.

Burns, C. and Myhill, D. (2004) 'Interactive on inactive', *Cambridge Journal of Education*, 30: 379–90.

Chomsky, N. (1965) *Aspects of the Theory of Syntax.* Cambridge, MA: MIT Press.

Cohen, N. (1996) 'Unsuspected language impairments in psychiatrically disturbed children: developmental issues and associated conditions', in J.H. Beitchman, N.J. Cohen, M.M Konstantareas and R. Tannock, (eds), *Language, Learning and Behaviour Disorders: Developmental, Biological and Clinical Perspectives.* Cambridge: Cambridge University Press.

Cortazzi, M. (1997) 'Classroom talk: communicating within the Learning Relationship' in N. Kitson and R. Merry, (eds), *Teaching in the Primary School: A Learning Relationship.* London: Routledge.

Cross, M. (2005) *Communication and Behaviour Problems*. London: Sage.

Crystal, D. (1994) *The Cambridge Encyclopedia of Language*. Cambridge: Cambridge University Press.

Cummins, J. (2003) 'Bilingual education: basic principles', in J. Dewaele, A. Housen and Li Wei, (eds), *Bilingualism: Beyond Basic Principles*. Clevedon: Multilingual Matters.

Dale, P.S. (1976) *Language Development: Structure and Function*, (2nd edn). New York: Holt, Rinehart and Winston.

Diorio, D., Viau, V. and Meaney, M.J. (1993) 'The role of the medial prefrontal cortex in the regulation of hypothalmic-pituitary-adrenal responses to stress', *Journal of Neuroscience*, 13 (9): 3839–47.

English, E., Hargreaves, L. and Hislam, J. (2002) 'Pedagogical dilemmas in the National Literacy Strategy: primary teachers' perceptions, reflections and classroom behaviour', *Cambridge Journal of Education*, 32 (1): 9–25.

Erikson, E.H. (1963) *Childhood and Society*. New York: Norton.

Ewers-Rogers, J. (1992) *Very young children's understanding and use of numbers and number symbols*. Unpublished PhD thesis, Institute of Education, University of London.

Frazier, I. (2001) 'Narrative modes of thinking applied to piano pedagogy', *Piano Pedagogy Forum, 4*,(2): **www.music.sc.edu/ea/keyboard/PPF/4.2/4.2.PPFpp.html**.

Freire, P. (1972) *Pedagogy of the Oppressed*. London: Penguin.

Freud, S. (1960) *A General Introduction to Psychoanalysis*. New York: Washington Square Press.

Goodenough, F.L. (1931) *Anger in Young Children*. Minneapolis, MN: University of Minnesota Press.

Hardman, F., Smith, F. and Wall, K. (2003) Interactive whole class teaching in the National Literacy Strategy. *Cambridge Journal of Education*, 31: 11–23.

Hargreaves, D. and Hargreaves. L. (1997) 'Children's development 3–7: the learning relationship in the early years', in N. Kitson, and R. Merry, (eds), *Teaching in the Primary School: a Learning Relationship*. London: Routledge.

Hayward, G. and Fernandez, R.M. (2004) 'From core skills: fast forward or back to the future?', *Oxford Review of Education, 30*(1): 117–45.

Hogarth, T., Shury, J., Vivian, D. and Wilson, R. (2001) *Employer Skill Survey 2001*. London: DFES.

Hunter-Carsch, M. (1999) *Report on the Leicester Summer Literacy Scheme*. Leicester: University of Leicester.

Kohlberg, L. (1966) 'A cognitive-developmental analysis of children's sex-role concepts and attitudes', in E.E. Maccoby, (ed.), *The Development of Sex Differences*. Stanford, CA: Stanford University Press.

Lees, J., Smithies, G. and Chambers, C. (2001) 'Let's Talk: a community-based language promotion project for Sure Start', in *Proceedings of the RCSLT National Conference: Sharing Communication*, Birmingham, April 2001.

Levinson, H.N. (1988) 'The cerebellar-vestibular basis of learning disabilities in children, adolescents and adults: hypothesis and study', *Perceptual Motor Skills*, 67: 983–1006.

Luria, A.R. and Yudovich, F. (1968) *Speech and the Development of Mental Processes in the Child*. London: Staples Press.

Mason, S. (1996) 'Table: 22 weak skills in the workplace', in *Skills and Enterprise Briefing*. London: DfEE.

Meadows, S. (1993) *The Child as Thinker: The Development and Acquisition of Cognition in Childhood*. London: Routledge.

Merry, R. (1998) *Successful Children, Successful Teaching*. Buckingham: Open University Press.

Miller, L. (2001) 'Shaping early childhood through the literacy curriculum', *Early Years: An International Journal of Research and Development,* 21(2): 107–16.

National Literacy Strategy (1998, 2001). London: DFES.

Nelson, D. and Burchell, K. (1998) *Evaluation of the Communication Opportunity Group Scheme*. South Warwicks, Combined Care NHS Trust, Department of Speech and Language Therapy, Warwick.

Parke, T. and Drury, R. (2001) 'Language development at home and at school: gains and losses in young bilinguals', *Early Years: An International Journal of Research and Development*, 21(2): 117–29.

Pertemps Survey (2004) *Employee Trends*. London: Confederation of British Industry.

Pollard, A. (1996) *The Social World of Children's Learning*. London: Routledge.

Pring, R. (2004) 'The skills revolution', *Oxford Review of Education,* 30(1): 105–16.

QCA (formerly SCAA) (1996) *Desirable Outcomes for Children's Learning*. London: HMSO.

QCA (1999) *Early Learning Goals*. London: DFEE.

QCA (2000) *Curriculum Guidance for the Foundation Stage.* London: DFEE.

QCA (2003a) *Speaking, Listening, Learning: Working with Children in KS1 and KS2*. London: DFES.

QCA (2003b) *Talking in Class*. London: DFES.

Sage, R. (1986) *A Question of Language Disorder*. MRC Trent Research Report.

Sage, R. (2000a) *Class Talk: Effective Classroom Communication*. Stafford: Network Educational Press.

Sage, R. (2000b) *COGS: Communication Opportunity Group Scheme*. Leicester: University of Leicester.

Sage, R. (2003) *Lend Us Your Ears: Listen and learn*. Stafford: Network Educational Press.

Sage, R. (2004) *A World of Difference: Tackling Inclusion in Schools*. Stafford: Network Educational Press.

Sage, R. (2006) *Communication Opportunity Group Scheme: COGS in the Classroom*. Leicester: University of Leicester Press.

Sage, R. and Cwenar, S. (2003) *The Escalate Student Feedback Project*. Leicester: University of Leicester.

Sage, R., Rogers, J. and Cwenar, S. (2004) *The Dialogue, Innovation, Achievement and Learning (DIAL) Project*. Research in England and Japan. Report 1. Leicester: University of Leicester.

Thompson, L. (1999) *Young Bilinguals in Nursery School*. Clevedon: Multilingual Matters.

Tizard, B. and Hughes, M. (1984) *Young Children Learning: Talking and Thinking at Home and at School*. London: Fontana.

Vygotsky, L.S. (1962) *Thought and Language*. Cambridge, MA: MIT Press.

Wang, M.C., Haertel, G.D. and Walberg, H.J. (1994) 'What helps students learn?', *Educational Leadership*, 51(4): 74–9.

Wilde, M. (2003) *Report on the Communication Opportunity Group Scheme with Pre-School and Talented and Able Groups*. Leicester: University of Leicester.

Wood, D. (1998) *How Children Think and Learn*. Oxford: Blackwell.

Wragg, E.C. (1994) *Managing Behaviour*. BBC Video and Book. London: BBC Publications.

Index

Tables are indicated by 't' following the page number